INEQUI A]

A CRITICAL OVERVIEW OF MONEY-MAKING,

MACRO-ECONOMICS AND PUBLIC PURPOSE

JUSTIN SYNNESTVEDT

The cover image

"Lazarus at the Rich Man's Gate" (1886), was painted by Russian romantic artist Fyodor Bronnikov, 1827-1892. Although perhaps an exaggeration of the 'Rich Man's' estate, it depicts well the Biblical text. The beggar was 'laid at his gate, desiring the crumbs that fell from his table, while dogs licked his sores'. (*Luke* 16: 20 – 31)

Foreward to the 2018 edition

In the four years since this book was published, the critical viewpoint it presents remains the same. The themes, historical trends, and my analyses and judgments about them, based on long study and personal experience, have not changed. Indeed, further research and observation have confirmed my views. I wish such ideas had also gained some increased attention – even legitimacy – in the popular corporate media – but that seems unlikely in the near term. However, a few high profile political figures, like senators Elizabeth Warren and Bernie Sanders, have brought progressive ideas about Modern Money Theory, and its relevance to fiscal policies into public discussion, especially during and since the 2016 presidential campaign in America.[1]

Religious and moral principles attached to debt don't change. Nor do the facts about the nature of money, and sovereign currencies, although people's understanding of them is notoriously fractious, and requires honest discussion of favored myths. Judgments about the role of government at every level in citizens' lives are clearly arguable. But few could favor the steady upward redistribution of wealth to the so-called 'One Percent' from all the rest, which harms most heavily those at the very bottom. This can't be a desirable social trend, nor does it help the economy 'as a whole'. Neither is it just an unfortunate result of the 'natural laws' of economics; there are no such laws.[2] These trends are the result of conscious decisions, by law makers, influenced by lobbyists and Wall Street 'experts', and sold to the public by media outlets whose jobs depend on the same oligarchic sources.

Political polarization, demands for austerity, clamor over deficit spending, protests demanding fiscal and social responsibility, are increasing. The 'financialization of everything' is more marked, and its negative consequences steadily increasing, on the U.S. economy and other economies around the world, both developed and developing, in what Michael Hudson calls "The Slow Crash" – i.e., the steady rise of *debt deflation*, where increasing debt forces people to reduce their consumption, which is the major driver of the U.S.

economy.[3] Breakaway movements, and the search for financial 'independence' are making international relations more fractious in Europe, threatening Greece, Spain, Scotland, and Britain, and stressing the larger economies of Italy, France and even Germany.

As I write this, the World Economic Forum of financial leaders from around the world are meeting in Davos, Switzerland, during which Oxfam released its statistics on world poverty. Approximately 82 percent of the money generated last year went to the richest 1 percent of the global population, while the poorest half saw no increase. The 2017 wealth increase of the roughly 2000 billionaires in the world is "enough to end extreme poverty 7 times over".[4]

Several recent books give further confirmation of the problematic trends my essay outlines. Michael Hudson's 2017 work *J is for Junk Economics*,[5] critiques the arcane and deceptive economic language used to keep people ignorant. Dean Baker's *Rigged: How Globalization and the Rules of the Modern Economy Were Structured to Make the Rich Richer* (CEPR: Washington, 2016) clarifies the financial world and its increasing political empowerment. John Kay's *Other People's Money: Masters of the Universe or Servants of the People?* (London: Profile Books, 2015) documents harmful changes in international banking and ways to correct them. Elisabeth Rosenthal's *An American Sickness: How Healthcare Became Big Business, and How You Can Take It Back.* (New York: Penguin Pres, 2017) shows the socially destructive effects of financialization on health and its delivery – a very current issue in American politics.

None of this is new, of course – only changing and intensifying. The 2016 U.S. presidential election was a shock to many people. However, from a long-term perspective, it can be seen as an unfortunate but logical consequence of the inequalities, and the frustration and anger they cause, compounded by general ignorance of the real reasons for social and economic discontents, which I've been observing and studying for more than forty-five years.

Chicago, 2018

Audience

I've written this essay for people who like to think rationally, in order to understand themselves and the world around them. It is for people who prefer a life of active self-development and useful occupation to one of conformity and comfort. It is for people who are aware that knowledge is not to be found in popular network news sources, nor will it come to those who prefer to believe ideas they are accustomed to, or that make them feel comfortable, or that help them fit into the social groups they want to join.

Summary

This book is a philosophical critique of debt and money-making in general terms, and an analysis of their changing role in contemporary American culture. It shows debt and money to be defined by social relations, rather than facts of nature, or precious commodities. It clarifies and reinterprets religious (Biblical) and ethical principles about debt and wealth. It discusses where control of the economy presently lies, and where it should lie. It summarizes the major concepts of Modern Money Theory (MMT), and how they can apply to our sovereign money system, and fiscal policies. And finally, it examines some conflicting views about the proper roles of government – especially central government – and why national concerns over debt need not prevent improvements to our quality of life.

Chicago, 2016

CONTENTS

To my mother, who taught me to love the Word,
and to love truth as the means to every good thing.

INEQUITY, INIQUITY

AND DEBT

For the poor shall never cease out of the land; therefore I command thee, saying, Thou shalt open thine hand wide unto thy brother, to thy poor, and to thy needy, in thy land. (Deut. 15:11)

For ye have the poor with you always, and whensoever ye will ye may do them good; but me ye have not always. (Mark 14:7)

It used to be no shame to be poor, but it was a shame to take charity.

Now it's a shame to be poor, but no shame to take charity. (Giacomo Andreacola – a fellow ditch-digger in my youth, and my mentor)

In the name of God and of Profit. (Francesco di Marco Datini, end of 14th C., inscribed on the ledgers of this Tuscan textile merchant)[6]

Chapter One

Introduction

Why I wrote this essay

Watching the bad behavior of our two political parties in the past four or five years, I'm reminded of the old-school parenting technique we used to hear about as kids. When two brothers carried a fight too far, their frustrated parent would stop it by knocking their heads together! Unfortunately, in a democracy, there no super-parent to impose order. What might be likened to such an authority in democratic society – 'The People' – can't bring the two parties into line this old-school way, because it is just as out of control as they.

Where can a rational person stand in the bitter political and social conflict dividing and disgusting citizens and elected officials alike, hobbling the government and damaging our international usefulness? What are the short and long-term consequences of this polarization for the society? Of course, it's natural to expect bickering over spending priorities in any democratic government, especially in the current context of an ongoing recession, a problematic financial sector, and record high debt, both personal and public. But beyond this, there are increasing systemic causes for division that need correction.

Should government help the unemployed, fight terrorism, provide health care, fix infrastructure, subsidize businesses, educate for high tech job skills, produce energy, improve the environment, or what? And to what degree? Where will it find the funds? Debt is said to be bad. How can it be paid off? *Austerity* is said to be the answer; in fact, it is the catch word. There is a broad popular consensus that taxes should be increased, to avoid a deficit, and that governmental spending should be decreased. The parties' fights are over which programs to cut, and whose taxes to raise. The political right and left have hardened their views. Judging by the sound bites of participants and comments of news broadcasters, extremism is the norm, and compromise is unacceptable.

Party politics has pushed aside practical solutions. Spokespersons for each group blame their opponents for the crisis of government. Everyone agrees there is no shortage of major issues for the nation, but the present state of dysfunction leaves them unaddressed and unsolved. Surely there must be better ways of framing questions, and solving difficult problems than what passes for political debate today. But despite this seemingly insoluble and untenable state of affairs, I've tried to develop some perspective on the noisy and sterile confusion, to analyze the uncivil character of the present dispute, and to point out some ways to reorient the discussion toward the public good.

Debt in America has been prominent in the news for nearly seven years. My interest in the subject was piqued by half a dozen topics – all related – that came to my attention more or less accidentally during that time. The first was an award-winning radio report in 2008 called "The Giant Pool of Money" – part of the *This American Life* series on National Public Radio – which explained the sources of the 2006 housing bubble.[7]

The second was the rise of the Tea Party movement and the extreme polarization of national politics during the 2010 election campaign. Third, a Thompson-Reuters white paper analyzed "Where

Can $700 Billion In Waste Be Cut Annually From The US Healthcare System?"[8] Fourth was Christopher Hedges' *Death of the Liberal Class,* which argues that traditional liberalizing institutions – academia, the press, the arts, government and even religion – have increasingly given in to money interests, rather than advocating for values other than money.[9] Hedges also notes that the Tea Party, which is part of a conservative movement which supports 'free market' capitalism, and hates federal financial regulation, paradoxically is also a reaction against the power of the financial sector in the economy and the loss of jobs which result from decades of unregulated Wall Street business, advocated by conservative policies.

Fifth, having heard a radio discussion of the history of banking and debt in America, I looked into the dispute between Hamilton and Madison about establishing a Federal Bank. This issue at the very beginning of our nation – when two famous 'Founding Fathers' argued their different views of democracy and the conflict between 'tyranny of the few' and 'tyranny of the many' – is completely relevant today, but few people know about it.[10]

I started writing this essay in an effort to understand the economics of debt and money, and to clarify and organize my ideas about issues that have caused so much national turmoil since the housing bubble burst in late 2006, triggering both the global financial crisis (GFC) in 2007, and the economic downturn that continues today. I have tried to get the biggest picture I could about the competing views of governmental 'getting and spending.' If my effort is successful, this analysis may help other people to make good personal and political choices about these matters.

The specific occasion for this undertaking was quite accidental. About a year ago I heard radio host Harry Shearer interview Stephanie Kelton on his program Le Show.[11] Kelton was explaining "Modern Money Theory" (MMT). It was a revelation! One might think economics has to be dry, but Professor Kelton's talk was fascinating. Modern Money Theory suddenly shined a floodlight on questions I've tried to answer more or less at random for many years – not just in the recent bad times. It offered a new way of looking at basic economic issues which are always present in the life of a nation.

Professor Kelton is a brilliant scholar and teacher, and very articulate. With a handful of other economists at the University of Missouri, and the Levy Institute at Bard College in New York, and a few associates in Europe and the UK, she has worked to establish a new understanding of modern money.[12] MMT is still outside the mainstream of contemporary economic thought that is popular in Washington and Wall Street (which, by the way, represents the views of politicians, bankers, and news commentators more than those of macroeconomists). Even so, MMT ideas have been gaining a foothold in the media and government circles, especially during the recent hand wringing over "fiscal cliffs," "sequestration," "grand bargains," "national debt," "austerity" and related jargon, which continues today.

I dislike class warfare, and partisan politics. Sad to say, both are more and more evident – often joined together – in the United States and other western nations. By "western nations" I mean primarily North America and Europe, which are democratic, capitalistic, wealthy, secular, technologically developed, and individualistic to a fault. Class warfare and partisan politics are also found in poor and undeveloped nations, and have been around for millennia. But where technology is highly developed, and popular media are open to everyone, and speech is uncensored, more and more people are influenced by false claims – today called "fake news" – and harmful attitudes, and pass them along. Class warfare and partisan politics are now the norm, while serious thought and civil exchanges are pushed aside.

Discourse in the American mass media tends to be strident, opinionated, unconsidered, and lacking any spirit of community or shared values. Critical thinking and good will are rare, and unlikely to develop in the foreseeable future, even though they would be much better mental habits to bring to any conversation, be it private and intimate, or directed to the widest public marketplace of ideas. By *critical thinking* I mean trying to get the biggest picture possible, and using reason to find what is true;[13] by *good will*, I mean simply using the Golden Rule in dealings with ones "neighbor" – whether she lives in the same house, or next door, or on the other side of the earth. Of these two mental habits, the latter (good will) is far harder to develop and far more important to practice. I make no special claim to it. As for the former, a long life of study and teaching philosophy has made critical thinking almost second nature for me, in most situations. All this is said only by way of apologizing in advance, if I fail to give fair expression to the issues dealt with here, which are both very old, and very current, and therefore very controversial.

The scope of this study has expanded as I learn more about the topic and its practical implications. Economics – especially macroeconomics – sounds terribly boring. But it's increasingly obvious to me that debt and money problems are not just matters for science and mathematics to solve. They are social issues, not only in how they affect people, but by their very nature. And being social, they involve the complexity of all human relations, including legal, moral and religious aspects. My work here has evolved into a critical overview of the history, nature and moral meaning of money-making, money and debt, and their current relation to the public good.

I've been thinking about societal problems for a very long time. My family used to discuss 'current affairs' over the dinner table. Fortunately, I grew up without television, which doesn't encourage viewers to *discuss* anything. It's largely addictive entertainment. So we read, and thought and talked. Hitler was about to impose war on the world when I was born, and the U.S. was poised soon after the war to become a major economic and military power of the world – capable of helping less fortunate people, at home and abroad, towards democracy and development. Those were times of worry, like now.

America and much of the rest of the world have seen great advances in my lifetime, especially in natural and social science, technology, medicine, civil rights and environmental awareness. Even so, there are serious weaknesses in what could be called our national psyche – problematic attitudes which increasingly hinder us from fulfilling our potential as a society, and as a force for good in other lands.

Some of these problematic attitudes are of long standing, and others have developed fairly recently, but all of them seem to be worsening. Of course, it's a matter of their degree and extent that makes them problematic. We see them in the growing distance between rich and poor, in degenerating public education, in racism and ethnic divisions, in intolerance of foreigners, and ignorance of other cultures, in arrogant and militant international relations, in the polarization of our interest groups, in our loss of community, in favoring image over substance, entertainment over growth, self-advantage over responsibility, and perhaps most obvious, favoring money over all other values.

I apologize for the number of topics this essay touches, many of which are proper subjects for lifetimes of scholarly research. My goal is an overview, to show how complex and interrelated are the topics that surround indebtedness, and to use this overview to bring their interconnectedness into focus. If I'm successful, this effort can serve to protect thoughtful readers from being comfortable with dogmatic assertions, which are everywhere around and inside us. We can learn to say, "Yes, but ..." as an antidote to that temptation.

The chapters that follow are intended as a philosophical critique of debt and money-making in general terms, and an analysis of their changing role in contemporary American culture. My essay shows debt and money to be defined by social relations, rather than facts of nature, or precious commodities. It clarifies and reinterprets religious (Biblical) and ethical principles about debt and wealth. It discusses where control of the economy presently lies, and where it should lie. It summarizes the major concepts of Modern Money Theory, and how they can apply to our sovereign money system, and fiscal policies. And finally, it examines some conflicting views about the proper roles of government – especially central government – and why national concerns over debt need not prevent improvements to our quality of life.

Chapter Two

Debts Are Social Relationships

Some etymology

The English word 'debt' comes from the Latin word *debere* which was shortened from *de habere* – to 'hold from' or 'take from' – i.e., something owed to another, either in the realm of human interactions or with respect to the gods. Connected to the idea of debt, we have the English words 'owe' and 'ought' from Proto Indo-European (PIE) origins, which show even more clearly both economic and moral or religious meanings. Actually, the word 'own' is a more basic form of both 'owe' and 'ought.' Originally 'own' meant 'master,' 'possessor,' or 'rich person.' (from which comes the name Owen). The idea that 'owe' and 'own' have the same origin seems strange, since in ordinary usage today they are almost opposite concepts. But 'owe' was originally a two-word phrase that meant "to own to give up" (i.e. to own temporarily), which was shortened to one word: owe. It's as though debt is passed along, so to speak, to some 'possessor' or 'master,' or even some ultimate creditor, to whom everything is owed.

This ambiguity is provocative, and reminds us of how multi-dimensional and important a place debt has always held. It is an ancient idea, and "modern debt" makes it seem especially difficult to understand and control, as I will show in later chapters of this study.

Debt is complex and scary

The topic of debt is enormously complex. The more I study it, the less certain I am of a full and valid general understanding. A big picture is the best I can hope for, and to express it well enough to be of some benefit to others. My difficulty is this: critical, or reasonable, or 'systematic' thinkers – as philosophers try to be – like to analyze and categorize subject matter, in order to see relationships among the parts – in terms of their scope, their cause-effect connections, their relative importance or value, etc. But debt resists such efforts at organization; the term covers so many kinds and characteristics.

Novelist Margaret Atwood wrote a fascinating and entertaining book about the darker aspects of debt as a wealth-gaining activity: *Payback – Debt and the Shadow Side of Wealth,* which inspired a film by the same name. [14] The book ranges widely over historical, cultural, economic and literary illustrations. If there is a theme in Atwood's book, it seems to be the importance of 'fairness,' which she discusses in the first chapter. Even so, I was left wanting a clearer understanding of debt, of how to distinguish 'good debt' from 'bad debt,' and especially of ways to solve the increasingly divisive and damaging social effects that wealth differences and indebtedness can have, as we see around us and around the world. These are questions I wish to look at here.

Debt is a social interaction

There are many kinds of debt: debts of gratitude (e.g. to parents, to God, to benefactors); moral debts (e.g. to speak the truth, to keep the Golden Rule, to refrain from violence); debts to society (e.g.

punishment for crime, public service, a "green" lifestyle); legal debts (e.g. paying bills, supporting children); and religious debts (e.g. following rituals, serving the mosque, church or temple); and of course, debts of material wealth. And these categories overlap.

Debts may be informal (e.g. by word, or a handshake), or more formal (e.g. a "slate" in the medieval tavern which was "wiped clean"); or they may be institutionalized (e.g. temple inventories in Mesopotamia, or state granted monopolies, or tax collection by the king's exchequer, or lending by private and public banks); and they may entail many nations and cultures (e.g. the Hanseatic League, or the International Monetary Fund). This brings up special problems which we will look at shortly.

There are public debts (taxes, or parking fines) and private debts ("Lend me a hundred dollars.") There are voluntary debts ("Buy savings bonds!") and involuntary (assessments for sewer construction). Some debts are secured (a home mortgage) while others are unsecured ("Can I borrow your dress shirt?") Debts may be incurred for receipt of property, or goods, or services, or money. Debts may bear interest or not. And interest-bearing debts need not entail money, as in sharecropping, or in trading spices for woven goods, with a 'cut' for the middle-man.

There is a time element to debt. Some debts have a specified term, while others may be indefinite ("In 180 days" or "Whenever you can"). Some may be incurred as "payable at the time of service." Some are very short term ("Wait here while I run into my house and get your fare," said to the cab driver). Some are very long term (e.g. life insurance, or a hundred-year lease). Even the idea of future and past get confused in some debt relationships. Is a religious 'sacrifice' made in payment for benefits already rendered, or as payment in advance to assure future benefits? And in the latter a case, who is the creditor: the one to whom, or the one by whom the sacrifice is made?

Some debts are 'paid forward', rather than paid back (e.g. when someone who has received a kindness 'passes it on' to someone else).

I like this idea, which involves offering help with no thought of repayment (let alone making interest on the deal), but of serving one's neighbor, or the general good.

Not all debts can be paid back. Perhaps the creditor dies, or the record is lost; perhaps the creditor is unknown (an "anonymous gift"); or perhaps the creditor has been paid by another party, even in advance. The Christian notion of redemption includes several of these conditions: Christ paid for others' debts; he paid them in advance; and he died before the debts could be repaid. I'll return to this idea below, when examining the religious meaning of debt.

When one thinks of the characteristics debts can have, the list seems endless. Moreover, the categories they suggest are not mutually exclusive; there is obvious overlap. As said before, the topic is very complex. However, there is something common to all of them; all debts are *social interactions.* This is important to keep in mind, but easy to forget, because the legal, institutional, international and 'econometric' aspects of modern debt are becoming more and more technical and specialized, and their social aspects can easily be overlooked. But if every debt is a social interaction, might it also be true that every social interaction is a debt of some sort? I've come to believe that, yes, indebtedness is an aspect of every social exchange (even the mere exchange of words), whether between individuals or groups. Let me clarify.

All social interactions involve indebtedness

There is some kind of *indebtedness,* or something analogous to indebtedness, in every social interaction – i.e. one party 'owes' the other something. One is 'enriched at the expense of another'. In every exchange one party ordinarily is (or is thought to be) more powerful, rich, superior, generous, kind, admirable, self-sacrificing, self-sufficient, independent, etc., than the other party, either before or as a result of the transaction. This is true even in an ordinary conversation

– a verbal exchange – which is a fundamental social transaction. Linguists know that speech has obligatory qualities – i.e. an indebtedness component. There are unstated (and typically unconscious, internalized) rules or conventions that determine how people must speak, or are expected to speak to each other in various contexts - i.e. what they 'owe' linguistically.

This obligation exists in terms of obeying grammatical rules or conventions, of course. If one breaks grammatical rules, it can damage her social status. She'll be thought ignorant. But more important are rules of common expectations and norms of politeness in speech, which are normally embedded in language use, but not typically thought of, or mentioned anywhere. For example, if someone meets you, and greets you, you feel obligated to respond; and the form of the response must be within tight limits of convention. If A says cheerfully to B, "Good morning! How are you?" and B answers, "Why do you want to know?", it will make A feel very uncomfortable. Maybe B is trying to put A on the spot – to change the social power relationship she has with A. We all do this unthinkingly.

With these ideas in mind, we might categorize all social exchanges, including ordinary debt relations, according to how their 'indebtedness component' is perceived by the parties to the transaction.

I think it's safe to say indebtedness is typical of all social interactions, but not necessary to them. An ideal social relationship may not – perhaps should not – entail any debt. Think about the story of Job, for instance. Does God 'owe' Job something, because of how righteous Job was, in keeping his side of the 'covenant'? Or is the 'obligation' entirely one-sided in favor of God? Perhaps one could make a matrix to understand and evaluate debts according to this 'indebtedness component', as it is perceived by the parties, and depending on how much "skin they have in the game". ('Skin in the game' reminds me of Shylock in Shakespeare's *The Merchant of Venice* – a classic debt relation.)

Personal and spatial distance in debt relations

Obviously debt entails debtors and creditors (or lenders and borrowers). That is, as said above, debt is a relationship and so can't be understood as distinct from that fact. Even so, many economists, business owners and accountants seem intent on studying debt as a 'thing' so to speak. Remember too that because debt is a social relationship, it has all the complexities of motive and circumstance that affect people. One of the most significant factors that may be easy to overlook is how distant, or impersonal debt relations can become. Moreover, as money becomes more and more (almost exclusively) not only the medium of exchange, but also the object of exchange, the depersonalizing separation between transacting parties increases, and the nature of that transaction becomes more and more abstract. Indeed, "money" as it exists today is largely an abstraction – an idea really – which is harder and harder to understand and control.

The idea of impersonality and distance in money economies is fundamental to, and inseparable from capitalism of every sort, but especially in modern financial capitalism. We will return to the meaning and role of "money" later in this essay. But it is useful to point out here a little realized fact about the development of capitalism in parts of the developing world, and in the areas which until recently were, or still are, 'socialistic'. Capitalism cannot work until the appropriate legal and social infrastructure exists that will support it. Crucial to this development is the idea of having verifiable legal documentation of property rights.

This notion of capitalistic infrastructure is the subject of a book by Hernando de Soto, *The Mystery of Capital.*[15] De Soto points out that people in non-capitalistic areas are not lacking in entrepreneurial spirit or skills. Their limitations come from the fact that they can't borrow money except from people within their communities who know them, and so who recognize whether they are to be trusted. They can be successful, have shops, own property, make trades locally, and have ideas that could well be developed to their own and the world's advantage, but they can't get the money – i.e. the 'capital' – because they don't have collateral which is formally recognized, recorded and guaranteed. If a person owns property or land that has been in the family for time out of mind, but lacks the legal documents to prove it, and a system of recording and accessing them, this property can't be used to guarantee the loan, except very locally.

The very thing that makes capitalism function on a large scale then is the thing that separates people in their borrowing-lending transactions. So the social meaning of debt becomes confused, the sometimes evil effects of it are often misunderstood, and the reactions to it are misdirected. As commercial and financial transactions develop internationally, and have a greater and greater place in people's everyday lives, the 'social' side of indebtedness becomes hidden and dark. People typically purchase goods and services whose price and availability they don't affect, from people who are totally anonymous and for all practical purposes, unknowable; and their borrowing and lending will often depend on financial transactions of institutions about which they are totally ignorant.

Indebtedness – degrees of freedom in exchange relations

I said above that it might be useful to see how exchange relations lie on a spectrum according to the degree of freedom or indebtedness which is perceived by the parties by whom the relationship was established. At one end, they are voluntary; at the other, involuntary. Looking again at the etymology of debt, we see the ambiguity of the Latin root *debere* which translates as 'owe,' 'have to' or 'must', on the one hand, and 'ought,' or 'should' on the other hand. This same ambiguity is found in Spanish, Italian and French (*deber*, *debere* and *devoir*). English has different words to distinguish what is more compulsory ('need to,' 'have to,' 'must') and what is more voluntary ('should,' 'ought.') So there is ambiguity in the concept of indebtedness, regarding freedom and necessity. Compare 'I need to eat something', or 'I have to pay the phone bill' with 'I should eat something', or 'I ought to pay the phone bill'.

Giving

Giving implies a sense of freedom, of course. It is 'voluntary'. We can imagine a 'pure gift' with no 'strings attached'. The giver is moved by affection or a desire to help or bring happiness to the receiver, but not compelled by obligation, or pity, or any sense of superiority, or the like. The receiver might, on one hand, feel compelled to accept the gift, from a sense of obligation to be 'gracious', but would not be comfortable. Or she might feel compelled to 'return the favor', and accept it with that in mind. But in the ideal case, the receiver might simply find happiness in the giver's expression of generosity, and feel grateful, but not obligated. These would be the unusual conditions of freedom for both parties. So we can see that 'giving' might, under ideal circumstances, be totally free of the 'indebtedness' element. One can say that this free relationship as an expression of love makes the ambiguity of 'own' and 'owe' become clear. The gift means that the benefit belongs to the beneficiary – it is his own; but at the same time the gratitude which is owed to the benefactor is expressed in love, and belongs to the benefactor – i.e. it is his own.

Taking by force

Taking by force is at the opposite end of the freedom – compulsion spectrum. A robbery is a forced exchange interaction, in several ways. The victim of course feels compelled to pay this 'debt' that the robber lays upon him. But the robber too may be compelled, psychologically. He may steal from a sense that he deserves to have the same goods that his neighbors have. If he feels superior to his victim in his own sight, he will tell himself that his victim (or the society) owes him the gratification of his desire. The victim in turn may think that the robber owes him a debt that eventually must be paid – a 'debt to society' or to himself. In addition to making good his loss, he may feel justified to exact 'interest' by violent means, even murder.

Slavery

Slavery is similar to robbery, for our discussion, but is infinitely worse. The debt of service is imposed upon the slave. The slave 'owes' (rather than 'owns') his or her work (and life) to the one who 'owns' him or her. Further, the slave owner may feel what he has taken is rightfully his, because the slave was a spoil of war, or was paid for, and so is 'owed' to him, and the future labor of the slave is part of that debt. Often the slave owner tries to pretend that the slave is not human, to lessen his sense of indebtedness or guilt. Needless to say, the slave may think the master is indebted to him, and that eventually he (or the gods of vengeance) will exact payment for the debt.

Neither of these two kinds of relationship above – the poles of giving freely and taking by force – is normally called a debt, but indebtedness may well be in the thinking of the parties nonetheless. More ordinary kinds of debt exchange lie on the same spectrum, according to how voluntary they are, and relatedly, how great is the sense of "indebtedness" for either of the parties involved. A person can perceive himself to be indebted, or think of another as being indebted to him. Keeping this in mind, let's look at some other kinds of debt, and their sense of indebtedness, in terms of freedom or constraint.

Religious ritual

Religious ritual is a kind of debt. The participants may enter voluntarily into it, as an expression of their gratitude to the higher powers, or the Divine, or they may feel compelled by fear of condemnation by their fellow believers or punishment by the object of their awe, if they fail to meet their obligations, whether in the forms of worship, or of sacrifice and offerings.

Wages for service or labor

Wages for service or labor is a debt relationship in which both parties owe something; they may enter into it willingly, or under the compulsion of need. The wage payer may offer work out of a sense of social responsibility, or as a way to benefit himself, for example as a holder of farmland, or a manufacturing or service enterprise. The laborer may be compelled to accept employment out of necessity to earn his bread, or he may seek the work because he loves it and appreciates his employer for providing an opportunity to do it. It is likely that both parties will feel a sense of indebtedness to the other, but not necessarily compulsion.

At the macro level, authoritarian states may employ all their citizens, assign them to various jobs, and pay them accordingly. Libertarian governments may leave employers and workers alone to find each other, and not be concerned if there are too few or too many workers for the labor market. Progressive governments may seek full employment, will probably regulate employer-employee relations, and may provide insurance for those who cannot find work.

Taxes

Taxes are debts imposed on members of a community by rulers. The one who lays the debt on the citizen (i.e. the 'creditor') may be a traditional monarch, a warlord or dictator, or a democratically chosen government. In no case are the citizens free to refuse to be indebted, but their sense of indebtedness might well be less in a democracy, because of their indirect input into the law through voting, and the benefits they perceive as a result.

Feudal agreements – pyramidal debt relations

Feudal agreements are a complex system of debts, which is particularly interesting because it entails levels of debt relations – in pyramid form. The ruler at the top places obligations on his subordinate nobles to provide military service and treasure and goods for his campaigns and other needs, in exchange for gifts of land, protection, and legal courts to settle disputes. The chain of mutual obligations and rights passes down to lower levels of nobility, governing smaller and smaller areas of land, and ends with lords who own farms and villages where food and goods are produced.[16]

As serfdom began to fade out in Western Europe in the late Middle Ages, it was expanding in Eastern Europe, where it lasted much longer – even into the 20th century (e.g. Russia in 1917). Reasons for this are outside the present essay, but obviously the development of both international trade and capitalism were affected negatively by feudal society. In Eastern Europe, neither international trade nor capitalism developed until after the demise of feudalism.[17]

The pyramidal system of debt relations, exemplified by feudalism, adds another characteristic of debt to our already complicated subject, which is relevant to contemporary debt conditions. We can see that as levels or circles of influence increase in the feudal system, more and more people are debtors, while fewer and fewer are creditors. It seems that modern debt takes on a similar pyramidal structure. Although many people in the middle tiers are both creditors and debtors, it seems that more and more people at the bottom are ultimately indebted to fewer and fewer creditors at the top of the pyramid. To me this also illustrates how the development of multinational corporate capitalism, and international banking (encouraged and aided by national oligarchies) encourages an increasing sense of indebtedness in society, and diminishes the freedom to avoid it. This has been leading to greater and greater social discontent and conflict. As I said above, the more distant in space, and the more impersonal debt relations become, the more social problems they entail.

"Trading"

Trade relations typically involve indebtedness, especially to the degree that there is distance between the trading parties, and there is a time lag in the exchange. In one-to-one exchanges, the term trade can be used loosely, as when a child says to her friend, "I'll trade you baseball card X for card Y". This transaction is typically right then and there – a straight 'swap' – and neither is indebted to the other. Each thinks she or he got what was hoped for, although upon further consideration, it might feel like a bad deal.

Trading in this person to person context becomes socially problematic when the parties don't know each other. Historically, a wandering merchant has been looked on with suspicion. The word 'gyp' reminds us of the social position of Gypsy traders, from the Middle Ages to today. Of course, that kind of debt may involve payback later on, if and when the Gypsy is ever seen again.

When groups trade with each other, there is a time and space element, which entails expectations of future interactions of giving and receiving. The idea of indebtedness may enter into such exchanges, although not in exact terms of what is owed. David Graeber, a British anthropologist, has written about the complicated and sometimes entertaining social interactions of various primal tribes he studied, centering on their wish to 'trade' with each other, but by no means objectively thinking about 'equal value,' or 'business only.' In these cases, there is no money to change hands, and even the goods which are exchanged seem to be of secondary importance compared to noneconomic social factors.

The actual 'trades' in the groups Graeber studied are typically dealt with in a last-minute rush, after a long day and night of dancing, drinking and apparently random sexual interactions, mock violence, and snatching desired goods out of one another's hands. These passionate and risky exchanges are a far cry from Adam Smith's notion, taken up by 'neoclassical' economists, of 'barter' by clearheaded, self-serving rational agents intent only on maximizing their profits, and therefore determining 'market values' and inventing money to 'lubricate' the transactions![18]

In contrast to these tribal interactions, which were mostly social, we have the development of the great international trading systems (e.g. the Phoenicians, Egyptians, Chinese, Indians and Romans), and the Medieval Italian cities, and the post-Renaissance colonizing nations of Europe (e.g. Portugal, Spain, England, Holland and France), whose purpose was almost exclusively the amassing of wealth. Debt, in the sense of making loans, taking interest, granting monopolies, etc. were part and parcel of these trade interactions, and the governments they represented, and helped to establish trade as long-lasting, formal and institutional. With the exception of oligarchs, whose influence is present in every state, personal relations became subordinated to the needs of the system. (We'll look at oligarchy in Chapter 5.) At the same time the social consequences of these systems were enormous; and individual citizens were greatly affected - by goods, services and labor that were needed for the trade, or were made available by the trade; as well as by prices, by wars, and by the great power successful traders had in their societies. This would be true, whether the traders were dealing only in goods (e.g. with the Phoenicians in the Mediterranean), or included letters of credit, bank exchanges, gold bullion and money (e.g.in the Venice spice trade with the orient).[19]

Pay off and pay back

Of course, pay, pay off and pay back are counter parts of debt. And as with debt, pay is also a social relationship. The word 'pay' has a wide range of meanings, both literal and figurative; obviously it plays an important role in our culture: pay a visit, pay one's respects, pay the bills, pay for mistakes, pay with one's life, it pays to think twice, pay out the fishing line, etc. These differing uses relate to differing kinds of indebtedness. We might expect that the 'economic' or 'monetary' meaning of 'pay' would be the primary one, and the other (more social) uses would be the derivative, metaphorical ones; but this isn't the case.

Etymology shows that the root origin of the word 'pay' in Latin (with earlier Indo-European forms), relates to *pacify*. More specifically, it means to impose peace by force. It's useful to realize that what we think of as money – a convenient way of making market exchanges – develops later among northern Europeans than among the trading businesses we've already mentioned.

The first uses of money to pay off indebtedness among ordinary citizens seem to have been the result of legal efforts to decide the proper 'recompense' for wrongs committed. 'You killed my brother. So you must pay for that.' Governments had to decide what was the appropriate 'pay,' to pacify the wronged party for acts that threatened to disrupt the social order. Pure vengeance was arbitrary, disruptive and unending. The use of 'money' to settle the payback issue was more orderly, objective and well defined. I put the term 'money' in quotes because these legal arrangements most likely were originally made with various kinds of material goods to 'make good' the debt to the offended party – like two camels, a piece of land, moveable property, or a daughter in the family.

'Weregild'

Weregild is a term for money payment made as recompense for taking the life of another (whether accidentally or intentionally) among Germanic tribes. It means 'man pay' (i.e. blood money), and was used widely in northern Europe from about the 4th to the 10th centuries, when it was replaced by the death penalty. The amount of the payment depended on the social rank of the victim. The lowest ranking 'freeman' was worth a 'base price' of about 200 *solidi*, and higher ranks were valued by comparison. A woman was worth twice as much as a man among some Germanic tribes (e.g. Alimani); but among the Saxons, she was worth half as much as a man. The Latin word *solidus* – 'solid' – refers to a gold coin weighing 24 carats. At the time of Charlemagne, one solidus was valued by law as equal to one yearling ox, or forty bushels of corn, or twenty bushels of rye.[20]

Just as debt comes in numberless forms, so there are numberless kinds of payment, depending on the culture, the nature of the debt and the particular circumstances of the debtor. People can pay or accept goods in exchange for services and vice versa. They can exchange finished goods for raw goods. Payments can be 'in kind,' or in money. A debtor may even pay with another person – e.g. a slave, or a child, or a wife – or himself as an indentured servant.

Pledges (Story of Tamar)

Pledges are tokens for indebtedness, like a down-payment - a minimal kind of security to show the obligation is taken seriously. The pledge has less value than the 'loan' it seeks. It can be material, or simply a matter of words, but it is formal, and holds a social power greater than simply stating an intention. This kind of payment is typical in cultures of honor, such as feudal societies, where keeping one's word is a mark of superior status; or where religious laws raise the consequences of going back on one's word. A pledge may be an object of value. A man might give a ring to his loved one, as a promise of marriage. "Earnest money" is often given in negotiations for a home sale, to show sincere intent to purchase; this will convince the seller to hold the sale for the would–be buyer.

A touching story in *Genesis* illustrates several points I've been discussing, set in a male dominated religious culture where women had little control over debt relations. Tamar was the daughter-in-law of Judah, the fourth son of Jacob. Judah was the father of the tribe from which David descended, and from whom the Jews are named. Judah married a Canaanite woman who bore him three sons. The eldest son, Er, married Tamar; but he "was wicked in the sight of the Lord, and the Lord slew him." According to custom, Judah told the second son – Onan – to "go in unto thy brother's wife, and marry her, and raise up seed to thy brother." (*Gen.* 38: 8) Instead, he "spilled it on the ground, lest that he should give seed to his brother." For this offense against family law (from which the term onanism comes), God killed Onan too.

According to custom, Tamar then expected the third son – Shelah – would take her to raise children, but Judah said Shelah was too young, and she must wait, a widow in her father's house, until the boy was grown. When it became apparent that Judah was not going to keep his word, Tamar dressed as a temple prostitute (with face covered), and when Judah passed by and noticed her, he asked for her favors.

> And she said, What wilt thou give me, that thou mayest come in unto me?
>
> And he said, I will send thee a kid from the flock. And she said, Wilt thou give me a pledge, till thou send it?
>
> And he said, What pledge shall I give thee? And she said, Thy signet, and thy bracelets, and thy staff that is in thy hand. And he gave it her, and came into her, and she conceived by him. (*Gen.* 38: 16-18)

Judah sent the promised goat by a friend, but the "temple prostitute" Tamar could not be found. Three months later, Judah was told that his widowed daughter-in-law was pregnant, and he ordered that she be brought out and burnt.

> When she was brought forth, she sent to her father-in-law, saying, By the man, whose these are, am I with child: and she said, Discern, I pray thee, whose are these, the signet, and bracelets and staff.
>
> And Judah acknowledged them, and said, She hath been more righteous than I because that I gave her not to Shelah my son. And he knew her again no more. (*Gen.* 38: 25, 26)

Pawns

Pawns are another kind of payment to secure a loan. Whereas a pledge typically has less value than the loan it secures, a pawn's value typically exceeds the loan it secures. Once again, the etymology here underscores the social origins of such a relationship, rather than its more contemporary 'cash meaning.' The word "pawn" in English refers both to an item taken to secure a loan, and to a piece in a chess game. Surprisingly, the more basic meaning relates to the game. The word relates to *peon*, which in Spanish (as in English) indicates a peasant farmer, or low-level worker. It further derives from the Latin word for flat foot or foot-soldier. A pawn in the chess-game, like the soldier in the feudal game, is expendable – the one who's labor supports and guarantees the success of the nobles managing the war.

Today we think of pawn shops as informal institutions for the down and out in society – a last resort for those whose circumstances don't allow them to get a bank loan. It's true that pawn shops serve neighborhoods where poor and shadowy characters live, and provide an easy way for thieves to turn their loot into cash. (St. Nicholas is the patron saint of both thieves and pawn brokers). But in some eras pawning became big business, lending money on a large scale to socially important clients who were not normally dependent on cash transactions. The Medici family of Florence, who became wealthy as wool merchants, and later as bankers, were also pawn lenders. In fact, the sign that hangs outside most pawn shops – three gold balls – is thought to be taken from the coat-of-arms of the Medici family, and may have been a three-dimensional version of three gold coins in their heraldry.

On occasion, even those at the very top of society might need to pawn their valuables to secure their immediate need for resources. Edward III of England (14th century) amassed a huge treasure, but he still had to borrow great sums from Florentine banks, a couple of which were bankrupted in the process. Immediately after his death, much of Edward's treasure was pawned by his grandson Richard II, to pay for further wars in France.[21] So although foot soldiers may be expendable pawns, they must be paid, along with other service providers to a military campaign.

Summary

The examples of debt given above lead to the following conclusion about indebtedness: To the degree that people are compelled to enter into debt relationships, and to the degree of burden of debt in those relationships (whether material or emotional), including that the debt seems to be increasing (as credit-card balances, student loans, immigrant sex-trade work, and underwater mortgages do) – then to the same degree one can say debt is onerous and destructive of societal wellbeing. These negative characteristics of indebtedness are prominent in contemporary society, as I'll try to make clearer in what follows.

Chapter Three

Capitalism and Modern Debt

Capitalism (mercantile, industrial, financial)

Many of the older kinds of debt sampled above still exist. But most debt today has characteristics that are quite modern – generally within the last one hundred years, and in case of the most onerous developments, within the last three or four decades. I'll examine these from the more general to the more specific, under several headings: capitalism, corporations, marketing, globalization, consumerism, new investment 'instruments,' and the F.I.R.E. sector.[22]

We've heard the term capitalism so often that it's easy to assume we know what it means. In my experience, few people who aren't economists or philosophers are comfortable trying to explain it, except to use a few undefined phrases, like 'free enterprise,' and 'competitive markets.' For the fans, 'capitalism' is a term of pride and allegiance, used to contrast with other societies who are 'socialists' or 'communists.' It's also used to put one domestic political group in opposition to another, who are called 'liberal' or 'communistic', or 'unAmerican' insofar as they are perceived as critical of capitalism. For my purposes here, it will be enough to point up a few aspects of capitalism that relate to the notion of debt and the public good. The picture will be very much simplified, and limited, but I think helpful in making judgments.

When thinking of capitalism, it seems too limited (and even narrow-minded) to concentrate on Northwestern Europe (and its North American offspring), and even there only in the last few centuries, given the several thousand years of systematic global trade relations and worldwide money transactions which went before. But it is the version of capitalism associated with western culture that has come to dominate the world's thinking and behavior for better or worse – i.e. a culture that combines capitalism with Protestantism, individualism, science, materialism and democracy (not all of which fit comfortably). But keeping the biggest possible picture, historically and globally, will help us know how we got to this place, and give us insights into what are good and bad decisions for the future.

History

Capitalism has a very long history, and it has changed radically from time to time. Without getting into scholarly historical debates, it seems safe to say the first 'phase' of capitalism was the development of exchanges among tribal groups, such as the people of Abraham and their neighbors (the "gentile" nations); or trade among cities, as in Phoenicia or in Rome; or international trade among states, and state sponsored associations (like the Dutch or British East India companies). We could call this first phase *"Mercantile Capitalism."* Next there was *"Industrial Capitalism"* of the sort developed in the late 18th century in England, after the advent of steam power, mechanization and knitting mills.

Finally, there is *"Financial Capitalism,"* which developed in the mid-20th century. This entails making conglomerates of companies and industries under larger and larger groupings or 'holding companies,' such as Standard Oil, Bell Telephone, Beatrice Foods and the Tribune groups, as well as investment banking, insurance, and other so-called 'financials,' whose main purpose is to maximize profits rather than make the enterprises competitive. Such companies don't 'make' anything; they 'own' things, which they buy and sell, combine, recombine, and reorganize. Financial capitalism is the increasingly characteristic trend in developed economies today – especially since around 1970. Factors that have entered into this development are diverse, and won't be dealt with here; they include expansion of the military-industrial complex; social movements toward 'freedom' with regard to race, personal life style, gender, political activism, and popular media; removal of the gold standard; loosening of banking regulations; the United States becoming the center of world trade (import) markets; the technology boom; the disappearance of the Soviet Union, *et al.*

Capital

Secondly, capitalism is based on the idea that to make wealth, one needs 'capital,' both to start, and to continue, an enterprise. For instance, it's not enough to sell, say, the woven goods I make on my loom. I must get people to buy my goods instead of my fellow weavers' goods. But to do that, I need to make the price, or quality, or attractiveness of my goods better than theirs. This entails that I use part of my 'income' to enlarge, improve and develop my weaving; I turn it into a 'business' instead of a 'trade.' The wealth or material I put into 'growing' my enterprise is called 'capital.'

With the need or desire for capital the idea of debt enters into the picture – psychological as well as material debt. I may have a sense of indebtedness because I am not wealthy or successful or powerful compared to those I want to emulate. Or I may actually be obligated to pay back debts which cannot be paid back by my presently available means. Or, I may borrow the means to improve my weaving enterprise, and go into financial debt in the process. That is, of course, the usual procedure of modern 'start up' companies.

Competition

A third aspect of capitalism is its competitiveness – which has obvious social effects. If I am in a guild of shoemakers, there may be a spirit of collaboration, as well as a feeling of playing an important role in the community. I might even help contribute to putting a stained-glass window in the cathedral, and as an advertisement, it might include a shoemaker adoring the Blessed Virgin. In a capitalist society, competition will overcome the spirit of community.[23] When I decide to 'go capitalist,' I look on other shoemakers as competitors; my success depends on their failure. I compete for 'market share' by driving them out of the market – completely if possible.

Monopoly

The last point brings up a fourth characteristic: capitalism is monopolistic. Paradoxically, the competitive spirit, together with the motivation to increase wealth without limit, results in the fact that capitalism tends towards monopoly, which will eliminate competition, if allowed to run its course. This is obvious from history. Monopolies were commonly given to Roman senators in the days of Caligula and Nero, and in Greece as far back as Aristotle's time (4th c. BCE) states imposed monopolies on scarce or vital products and processes. The opportunities for corruption are obvious, and continue today. Over and over, capitalist societies have suffered the ill consequences of monopolies, and have taken whatever steps seemed necessary to control or eliminate them.

Corporations/ LLCs

A fifth aspect of capitalism is its connection to law, or societal control. Like much else we have been looking at related to debt, the history of corporations is very old, and misty, and widespread around the world; scholars are by no means all in agreement about it, even in its more recent and limited forms of Medieval Europe. But again, we can safely make some claims. Corporations are formal organizations. Their names and functions varied according to the time, the legal subtleties, and the language in which they originated. For example, Hanseatic league comes from German *hansa*, a military troop; guild comes from Norse *gildi* – payment; university comes from Latin *universus* – the entirety; cartel is from Greek and perhaps Egyptian *khartes* – papyrus leaf; borough is from Old English *burg* – fortified town, etc.

Corporations might be charters given to villages by regional nobles, permitting them to operate outside of the set of traditional feudal obligations that developed after, say, 800 C.E. They might be guilds of merchants, tradesmen, or artisans designed to protect and supervise the rules of business, commerce, or quality of work, and to protect their members and adjudicate disputes. They might be 'universities,' or religious schools, founded by church orders, or royal patrons, to insure standards and principles of education; or student unions which sought uniformity of curriculum and legitimacy of students' credentials. Or they might be monopolies granted to groups or even to favored individuals, to set up and carry on foreign trade, or production of important goods and services, if it was thought to benefit the rulers.

The word 'corporation' itself seems to be not as old as the other terms for 'legal bodies' mentioned here. It comes directly from the Latin *corpus* – a body. And as we know, it is the idea of making a group of persons into a single 'body', or citizen, and treating it in law as separate from any of its individual members. We could say a corporation has rights and obligations, like any citizen, but that is misleading. A corporation must pay taxes, and can be sued, but it can't be married, or put in jail, nor can one call it moral or immoral in any serious way. Corporation is a legal abstraction, which originated perhaps in the 15th century. But one famous historian of law – Harold Laski – pointed out almost a century ago, that we shouldn't try too hard to impose our modern view of incorporation on the very ancient forms of social, political and economic cooperation we have mentioned.

> The abstractions of early jurisprudence are post-conquestual in origin;[24] and we may even doubt whether the early communalism which has so much affected the economic speculation of our time is not in fact more truly individualistic than we care to admit.[25]

Governmental control – myth of 'pure' capitalism

The key point to remember is this: in every instance, location and time, the various corporate 'bodies' have always been legal entities, created by governmental authority, in order to benefit the government or the society. Incorporation was not, at any time, a right which every ordinary citizens could presume, to carry on whatever enterprise they wished, in whatever way they wished. For example, the contemporary notion of a "limited liability corporation" (LLC) is an agreement to provide some degree of security to the owners of an enterprise, so that they might develop their work without fear of being sued individually for its failures or even its negative social impact. But that protection (limited as it is) is granted in exchange for the benefit which the LLC (or any traditional corporation) is thought to render to the government or society, which rests on the judgment of the governmental authority.[26]

I think it is well to note that the idea of 'pure' (in the sense of uncontrolled or 'free' market capitalism) is a myth – one which seems to be encouraged by so-called neo-classical economists who presently have the most influence on US fiscal policies. Adam Smith (and his current followers) believed there are 'natural laws' – e.g. 'supply and demand' – which regulate the economic behavior of individuals, and keep capitalism in check. But history shows this is false, and the suggestion or implication that the 'free market' ought to be unregulated in practice is very foolish (as recent economic disruptions are proving). Actually, not all of Adam Smith's ideas supported the viewpoint of current neo-classical economics. He was, for instance, a harsh critic of the 'rentier' class who, he thought, did not contribute to the social good, but benefitted simply by being owners.

Harvard Professor Bruce Scott deals with some of these points in his 2009 book, *The Concept of Capitalism*. This very readable and short work (seventy five pages!) is a summary of a major study he has since published about the history and evolution of capitalism.[27] He wanted to get some of his core ideas into the debate leading up to the 2010 election. Scott makes an analogy between economics and professional sports. In both, there are 'rules of the game.' Players must play according to the rules, but periodically the rules are changed when circumstances or interests require it. So society sets the rules according to which capitalism may be played by the participants, and when it sees fit, it can favor one party, or product, or permit limited monopolies, etc. As I said before, the free market does not now exist, and never has existed, and that is appropriate. For the most part, the rules that limit capitalism involve a contest between governmental regulations, which in principle (though certainly not in practice) represent the public purpose, and a few private players, who have always managed to manipulate markets, public opinion and governmental policies in their favor.[28]

Contemporary problematic trends

Capitalism is growing, of course. As the world's population grows, and undeveloped and underdeveloped areas begin to move from traditional to modern forms of society, they are well aware of material advantages they see in the developed world – education, technology, health care, social freedoms, gender equality and the rest. It's natural and appropriate that they are attracted to the market economies which can harness their entrepreneurial skills, and bring these benefits. It would be well indeed if they could manage this, while avoiding some of the excesses that have been taking the shine off our own economy in the past several decades, which I'll discuss below.

Each people has its own national problems and character, so development will differ from place to place. We might benefit from deciding which traits of American capitalism and society would export well to other countries, and how they could best be applied in different cultures. I recommend a Nobel Prize winning book on this topic – comparative development – by Amartya Sen, *Development as Freedom.*[29] Typically there are conflicting views both inside and outside of each developing country on the best way to bring development about. Sen's main point is that money should not be the focus of development efforts, contrary to popular views. Instead, development should begin with various freedoms, taken in the broadest sense, such as good health, good education, gender equality, and political participation. These things do not require a lot of money, and they will lead to a better life right away. Economic development will follow these other phases of development naturally. I bring this up, because the idea seems to apply to our own country as well – especially to the parts of our society which have been increasingly left 'undeveloped' by the new problematic trends in our own version of capitalism.

Globalization, multinationals and trans-nationals

It is nothing new that corporate capitalism has a global reach. That was true of the great trading systems in antiquity, and increasingly so in Europe throughout Medieval, Renaissance, colonial and modern times to the present. The difference, we could say, is one of scale. But as is often suggested by historians, there are times when quantitative changes seem to bring about qualitative changes as well. New goods and new ideas are introduced to societies by traders, of course. But at times, the character of a society may shift to being, e.g. a provider of 'raw materials,' like lumber, cotton and iron ore; or of 'desirable goods,' like tea, bananas, diamonds, gold or slaves. Obviously these involve radical shifts in the societies of both trade partners. And needless to say, there is typically an imbalance of advantage, in favor of the more developed trader.

These are old issues. Generally global trade can be seen as helpful, insofar as it provides opportunities for development to the less developed societies, in terms of higher income, better health, education and environmental improvement; or harmful, in terms of sweatshop labor, 'monocrop' agriculture, political corruption or environmental degradation. Usually there is a trade-off; it's not a black or white situation.[30]

In recent decades, many corporations have become multi-national – i.e. they operate in more than one country. In 1970, there were 7000 multi-national companies; in 2006 there were 78000, the great majority of which are in the developed countries, and in the northern hemisphere.[31] Globalization hasn't been a uniform case of a rising tide raising all ships. In terms of wealth, for instance, the per capita income difference between rich and poor nations was ten to one in 1900; that difference in 2000 had risen to sixty to one.[32]

We often hear of the "global village,," which is a friendly sounding term. It seems to mean that because of staggering developments in communications technology, people around the world can instantly be in touch. That is true, but the closeness can be problematic. Ideally, understanding what is going on around the world is a mind-expanding experience. Like travel or study, international communications can help us to get a big picture of people, and help us lose some of our natural parochialism. We can begin to see that all people share a common humanness, regardless of their differences, which ought to help us treat others with fairness and respect. We're all brothers and sisters in 'the global village'. That sounds wonderful. But on the other hand, by reason of global marketing, trade and communications technology, many people are brought under the influence of the shallow trendy tastes and material values that represent the European, and especially American popular cultures. Their own cultures, and their own real villages – not the 'global village' – come under threat of ridicule or destruction. We need to remember that people are both all the same, and all different.

Trans-national corporations add another dimension to the problems of international trade, primarily to the degree that they are not linked to any particular national government. For that reason, they are more free to work around public controls (e.g. of wages, taxes, work conditions, environmental laws, and other possible limits to their success), to encourage or take advantage of corruption, and to have more competitive power against corporations whose reach and influence is not so great.

Marketing

Although markets and trading have been around since civilization began, the idea of "marketing" as an area of study and expertise is recent. Looking briefly at this topic may help us understand yet another dimension to modern debt. The term 'marketing' came into English about 1884.[33] So it was a distinct idea in circulation at that time. Marketing became a subject for serious study when the University of Pennsylvania devoted a course to it in 1905; and it was part of the curriculum in the first school devoted to business at Harvard University in 1908.

Like so many other aspects of debt in society, marketing has become hugely influential in recent history, and has exploded in recent decades. The following are some innovations in marketing history.

Radio advertising started in 1922; 'telemarketing' came in the Fifties; 'data based' marketing techniques became the norm in the Seventies, and 'e-commerce' began at the same time; 'customer relationship management' (CRM) developed in the Eighties; and 'integrated market communications' (IMC) together with CRM have been increasingly the norm since the Nineties. The first academic institute for research in this subject – The Centre for Integrated Marketing – was set up in 2002, at the University of Bedfordshire, England.

Obviously, each of these steps is closely related to developments in communication technology. Equally obvious, the economic and social effects of marketing, here and around the world, can be good or ill. I'm sure motivations of those who understand and use modern marketing methods are no different from those of marketers a century or even millennia ago. But the power of these methods to effect changes on the way people live and think – on their material and mental cultures – has multiplied beyond measure.

'Targeted advertisement' is one way of making marketing more cost effective. Instead of making a general appeal, advertisements address a specific group of potential customers where the persuasion can be more focused. An example is the National Football League's campaign to build a future fan base by targeting children. Since 1995, the NFL has collaborated with Nickelodeon – a children's television cable channel – to produce a series of animated short video programs, including "NFL Rush Zone: Season of the Guardians," in which well-known football players take on animated personas, and speaking roles, in various fun adventures about bad guys being kept from achieving their nefarious designs.

A more specific – in fact individualized – targeting occurs when people who use e-mail on smart phones or computers see pop-up ads appearing on their screens, for products that exactly correspond to the topics of the emails they are sending or receiving. This is true for purchases of, or inquiries about certain products; but presently the content of personal emails is still secure, except from government authorized inquiries.[34] If I do a web search, or visit a page for information about a vacation trip to Chile, or research medical data about an inflamed tendon, ads might appear about travel agencies, or anti-inflammatory medicine. Uncanny!

The moral status of marketing

The kinds of marketing mentioned above seem, at the least, to be invasions of privacy; they are certainly intrusive. In the case of targeting children, they begin to look like violations of moral rules. The terms 'campaign' and 'target' as used by advertising personnel suggests a militant perspective, which matches invasions (of privacy, or of cultures, or even 'economic war' against competitors). I mention this because it could be argued that marketing, and the indebtedness that results from it, are kinds of violence that the spirit of capitalism can unleash, with harsh economic and social consequences. I raise this issue because it has often occurred to me that the very idea of marketing is morally problematic. I won't discuss the various problem areas mentioned above, which are frequently discussed by advocates and critics of global capitalism. I can however deal with one very broad ethical question that interests me. It can be argued that marketing itself is questionable morally, because *it violates people's freedom to judge what is good or important*. Let me explain.

Every marketer tries to get customers to bring their money to the business he or she serves, rather than to the competitors. He must convince the customers that it is to their benefit to do so. He can either lie to, or manipulate, the audience to accomplish this. It is typically against the law in developed countries to make false claims in advertising, so ads don't often lie directly (although every degree of misleading seems acceptable). But the main emphasis is on controlling the customers' choices through psychological manipulation of every sort, whose mastery is the work of highly paid agencies. The common claim that individuals are 'free to make choices' is demonstrably ridiculous. Proof lies in the great success of marketing efforts. But even if a particular ad, say for Brand X Beer, doesn't have the power to force person Y to choose that brand (presuming she is going to buy beer, of course), the impotence of the marketer to accomplish his aims does not excuse his efforts to control the choice.

In his *Groundwork of the Metaphysics of Morals* (1785), Immanuel Kant gave this famous moral command: "So act in such a way that you treat humanity, whether in your own person or the person of another, never merely as *a means to an end*, but always at the same time *as an end*." By 'humanity' Kant meant any person, i.e. one who has the ability to decide for herself or himself what is valuable or good. That ability to *judge value* is the source of all value; nothing is valuable unless a person chooses to think it is. There may be differences of judgment, of course, which depends on both the intellect (for finding the moral truth), and the will (for committing to it). So a person's ability to choose what is valuable or good is itself good; in fact it is the essence of 'humanity.' (Of course, if the person is a child, or weak minded, a responsible adult must choose what is good for the one who cannot do so for himself.) It follows that any effort to take away a person's ability to decide and choose what is good, and impose one's own idea of good on that person, strikes at the meaning of what it is to be a person; that is immoral, even if the person agrees to it. This control can be by coercion, or by deception. Either way, it does evil to that person. This is the case, even if the controlling agent has the best of intentions. But in the case of advertising methods, the motives are clearly not the best of intentions; they are to use the customer for the benefit of the marketer.

Against this argument, it could be claimed that consumers are only 'getting what they want'. So they are not coerced, it is said. Perhaps that is true. I don't think it is a marketer's job to give clients or the society what is good for them. Nor am I naïve enough to think there is a big market for 'public service' ads. Nor can it be reasonably suggested that the role of businesses is to improve public morality, education or health. That's all obvious. But on the other hand, it does not seem morally 'neutral' when businesses promote childish self-interest, immediate gratification, and expectations of pleasure, popularity and success to anyone who gets the latest application for the newest cell phone, or the coolest running shoes. This is to say nothing about the 'goods' that are marketed which actually harm people, like addictive sports drinks, fast foods, pornography, and easy credit (read 'easy debt').

"Consumerism"

Another problem area of modern debt relations (commerce and trade) is consumerism. The consumerism I have in mind is the very recent rise of a social attitude that conceives of 'buying' or 'consuming' as a shared societal value. This goes beyond normal motivation, and becomes threatening to the mental health of a society.

Of course, people's desires have always run ahead of their means. And if the means are available, people will often go beyond what is good for them. Socrates discussed this twenty-four centuries ago, in Book II of *The Republic*. We see it also in the decadent periods of the Roman Empire. A century ago, sociologist Thorstein Veblen identified a third kind of consumption – "conspicuous consumption" – among the upper class, as a status symbol.

These attitudes towards consumption all still exist, but 'consumerism' adds another dimension to the contemporary picture. Consumerism today is a widespread attitude, which goes across class categories, and becomes part of mass culture, including the underclass. It is the popular belief that buying things is proof of one's personal worth, as well as providing a sense of community. Distinct from earlier attitudes about spending, consumerism doesn't set the 'haves' apart from the 'have-nots' so much as give everyone a false sense of belonging and social security. The things that are bought are often not even used. It is the buying, and the talk about it that are important, more than the using, or even the 'having'. People report feeling better when they can 'go shopping,' which usually means walking through a mall with no particular purchase in mind, and no particular need, but with the intention of making a purchase if it looks good, or seems to be a bargain. Needless to say, this is all very pleasing to merchants.

Venture capitalism, speculation, and Ponzi schemes

Another problematic aspect of modern debt relationships is the rapid invention and deployment of new 'instruments' for wealth generation. Their variety is great, and the techniques for their use are sophisticated, requiring complex business models and computer technology. But their rapid development and success in the hands of some investors is also their major drawback; they have developed too quickly to be understood broadly in terms of their risks or possible social damage, and they have not been suitably controlled by laws or regulating agencies. Among these are the combining of ordinary lending and speculative investment functions of banks; high degrees of leveraging of bank funds with little regard for safe levels of reserves; using credit-default swaps to insure investments; selling 'tranches' (slices) of bundled assets to second- and third-hand buyers, who are unaware that they may be backed, e.g., by worthless mortgages (now called 'toxic assets); investing enormous amounts of capital in very low yield products, and using computer analysis of 'risk' based on questionable data, and overoptimistic expectations of market trends, etc. All of these behaviors in the so-called FIRE sector of the economy went awry in 2006, bringing on the global financial crisis (GFC) whose consequences are very much still with us, as we discussed above.

Many of these investment strategies were used in response to the recent enormous increase in money 'looking for a place to be invested' – a global pool of so-called "fixed income securities" that doubled in just six years, from $36 Trillion (in 2000) to $70 Trillion (in 2006). The 'Giant Pool of Money'[35] came mainly from rapid economic growth in poorer countries like Russia, India, Abu Dhabi, Saudi Arabia and China. This put great pressure on investment bankers and others to find financial 'products' to sell to the managers of this huge pool of money that would seem quite safe and attractive. Since the housing market had been booming, investment bankers used home mortgages to 'back' the 'secured' products they offered to the money pool investors. But the supply of mortgage money ran out, so mortgage sellers began a campaign to sell mortgages as fast as possible, with little or no attention to collateral, job security or income to justify the sales; while on the other side, eager would-be home owners bought mortgages on which they were almost certain to default.

The financial bubble burst when the over-built housing market began to lose value, which triggered an international financial crisis, with a loss that could amount to about $12 Trillion. This is a fifth of the world's total economic activity.[36] This is a prediction of the total costs that may occur. Bank costs have been calculated at about $4 Trillion following the near collapse and bailout of international banking as well.[37] My simplified summary doesn't even touch the varied types of speculative investments which were ongoing, whose degree of risk ranged from legal and quite manageable (like hedge funds) to illegal and guaranteed to fail ("Ponzi" schemes), with the majority of activity somewhere in the murky middle ground.[38] In response to the global financial crisis, governments involved have responded with various efforts to save their financial sectors, without much apparent regard for the larger pictures of their economies in general. Our government undertook a series of 'bailouts' of major financial institutions whose influence was thought to be great enough to suggest they were "too big to fail". Simon Johnson, a chief economist at the International Monetary Fund in 2008 and 2009, summarized some of this activity in a *New Yorker* article of May, 2009: "The quiet coup".

In March 2008, Bear Stearns was sold to JP Morgan Chase in what looked to many like a gift to JP Morgan. (Jamie Daimon, JP Morgan's CEO, sits on the board of directors of the Federal Reserve Bank of New York, which, along with the Treasury Department, brokered the deal.) In September, we saw the sale of Merrill Lynch to Bank of America, the first bailout of AIG, and the takeover and immediate sale of Washington Mutual to JP Morgan – all of which were brokered by the government. In October, nine large banks were recapitalized on the same day behind closed doors in Washington. This, in turn, was followed by additional bailouts for Citigroup, AIG, Bank of America, Citigroup (again) and AIG (again.).

The 'coup' which Johnson discusses is the way that principal figures of the financial world have come to dominate decision making at the U. S. Federal Bank and Treasury Department (often called the Wall Street Washington Corridor), with little or no congressional involvement or understanding, and that this connection works to the great advantage of the financial corporations and their officers, but to the disadvantage of the real economy. There are many critical and scholarly analyses of the course of governmental involvement in the financial crisis that began seven years ago, showing how hasty decisions, deception, inappropriate policies (or lack of policy), personal influences and self-interest have harmed the financial order of things, and left the economy in a major slump that may continue on for years, or at best come back slowly towards what it was.

Unfortunately, most of the scholarship gets pushed aside in the noisy political cage fighting and punditry of the popular media. The practical conclusion of Johnson's article is that America will not get its financial house in order unless, like all the IMF client-nations he has observed in financial crisis, it realizes that the problem lies "almost invariably" with the politics of the country, and does what is needed to correct that. Specifically, America, like any such nation in crisis, needs to break the control of the few persons at the top of the financial industry – the "oligarchy" – who are "running the country rather like a profit-seeking company in which they are the controlling shareholders."[39]

To exemplify the difficulty of reforming the system, take the Dodd-Frank Wall Street Reform and Consumer Protection Act –

signed into law about four years ago (July 2010). It has been steadily eroded by foot dragging, by legal challenges to every provision of the bill, by a steady marketing campaign to discredit it, and by law suits to reject it as constitutionally illegitimate, so that fewer than half its provisions have gone into effect. And this act has left untouched the problem of having banks that are 'too big to fail.' Presently these banks are even bigger than they were at the time the government undertook to bail them out with taxpayer funds, which were used to acquire new holdings, to recapitalize, and to give large bonuses to executives who were managing their policies which brought on the crisis. And their current operating procedures leave them just as vulnerable as ever to another crisis.[40]

To summarize this theme, the three most important lessons to be learned from the (still ongoing) global financial crisis so far are, first, to understand which types of investment can be sustained in a stable manner, and which ones tend naturally and necessarily to instability; second, to develop regulations and oversight as needed to protect the financial markets from abuse; and third, to insure that the nation's financial industry works for the economic benefit of the whole, and to give ultimate control of that industry over to transparent and democratic processes.

Growth of FIRE sector and the 'rentier' class

The last aspect of modern debt I find problematic is the rapid growth of the FIRE sector of the national economy, mentioned above – i.e., Financials, Insurance and Real Estate. In the Seventies, it represented about 4% of GDP, but generated about 16% of all corporate profits; and in the last decade (2007), it represented about 8% of GDP, while it generated 41% of all corporate profits![41] To give another view of the same phenomenon, by 2007, an average household paid more to the FIRE sector than it spent for food, beverages, transportation and utilities combined; which is 50% more than on health care, and 65% more than on building projects.[42]

Until very recently, the pay of corporate executives in the FIRE sector was comparable to those of other industries. But in the last decade, it has increased to almost twice that of other sectors. (181% according the Simon Johnson). It's intuitively obvious that this imbalance will result (and has resulted) in an increasing move towards financial industry occupations rather than to other sectors, for those who have the influence and means to manage it. This is problematic for several reasons.

The first problem is that a financially top-heavy economy is neither healthy, nor balanced, and certainly not 'humane'. It is often claimed that an economy is 'improving' if the GDP is increasing. That is not true, if the increase in wealth does not translate into an improvement of the society's quality of life. As someone quipped, GDP counts all the 'goods and services,' but also all the 'bads and disservices'. More importantly, perhaps, an increase in 'per capita income' doesn't count for much, if the 'average' income doesn't represent the 'typical' income – i.e. that most of the increase goes to a very few people at the top (which has been the case since 1970 in the United States.

It may well be that an economy which generates great wealth *could* provide the necessities of life to all its citizens, but that would depend on passing laws which distribute goods and services or even money to the lower classes, which is very unlikely. More importantly, though, even if that distribution of necessities were accomplished, lower class citizens would have little sense of making a real contribution to the society; they would all be 'kept' by the wealthy class, and would be beholden to them. An example of this was brought to my attention by my students from Kuwait in the Nineties, all of whom came on tuition grants given by their government, which was flush with oil income. None of the students could look forward to a job at home, after completing their education. They got the 'benefits', but no sense of having earned them. I don't think this is beneficial.

Relatedly, a financially dominated society does not employ people in the same way that a more balanced society would, in which people are rewarded for a variety of activities, in making goods and providing services for ordinary life. In a financial society, those goods more and more will be imported from other places, and many people will remain unemployed. Employment is a basic need for people; without it they are less than human, because their individual skills are not needed, nor their interests developed. Money is not a social goal; it is a means to provide commerce and growth and the opportunities for social contribution. Granted, this must sound too idealistic.

Furthermore, a finance-dominated society is not self-sustaining. So-called 'rentiers' gain their wealth by reason of laws which respect their right to 'own' property, and companies. They don't typically gain wealth by producing things, but by owning, organizing, grouping and regrouping, and selling off the companies which do produce things successfully. In effect, the more of the society's wealth comes from ownership, the less will come from production of goods and services that are beneficial to the society. The financial industry could be called parasitic on the non-financial industries, in the way some conservatives have called recipients of 'entitlement payments' parasitic; and its increase will gradually lessen the success of the rest of the economy. Of course, it is a matter of degree, and the term 'rentier' has long been used as a term of disparagement, as a general criticism of capitalism. Anyone who rents out an apartment, or holds a patent on the use of a product, is a 'rentier'. That's all right. Property ownership *is* basic to capitalism. The problematic character of current emphasis on the financial industry is a matter of over-emphasis, and the degree to which it takes from the development of goods and services that add to the 'real economy'.

Finally, as pointed out in the previous section, an economy dominated by money interests gives too much control into the hands of the wealthy oligarchy. The whole system becomes undemocratic, since the power of wealth can subvert the democratic process, and convince the governors (and the populace which elects them) to provide legal support for their continuing financial advantage as we will examine below.

Chapter Four

Debt, Wealth and Scripture

Scriptural principles about lending and debt

In the scriptures of the Abrahamic tradition (Jewish, Christian and Muslim), there are many, many references to debt in all its forms, and the attitudes and laws that should inform debt relationships and indebtedness. Some of these seem to deal clearly with business transactions, including the trade and sale of property, goods, services, and money. Others seem to be addressing specifically moral or 'religious' aspects of debt relations. It seems to me that this distinction is easy to see in western culture, because secular, 'purely economic' considerations are set apart from moral ones (and emphasized); this is not so obvious in Biblical scripture. There is a basic ambiguity in any 'religious' culture, because every aspect of life falls under the influence of religion. There is no separate secular life there. So scriptural texts that look to us like business talk are also metaphorically dealing with the 'business' of human relations; this is a point I have been emphasizing. In this chapter, I'll suggest an interpretation of some Biblical texts about debt from the perspective of their moral, religious and metaphorical meanings.

The first Biblical reference to lending I can find is in *Exodus*, where the Law is being given to Moses in detail: "If thou lend money to any of my people that is poor by thee, thou shalt not be to him as a usurer, neither shalt thou lay upon him usury." (*Ex.* 22: 25)

The word 'lend' here (*lavah*) has the root meaning of 'unite,' or 'twine,' reminding us that lending, whether for good or ill, is a strong (and typically emotion laden) connection. The conditioning idea is that lending to a poor countryman should not be 'as a usurer' (*nashah*), which means to lend with interest or security. The word 'usury' (*nehshek*) comes from *nashak,* which means 'bite' in its root: the painful bite of interest that comes with the loan.

I said this *Exodus* text is the first that deals with lending specifically. However, in the *Genesis* story of the Fall, the same word *nashak* is used when Eve tells God that the serpent 'beguiled' her. In other words, the spirit of deception and leading astray represented by the serpent is at the heart of lending to one who is poor and cannot be expected to pay back the loan without dire consequences. Behind this law is the idea that one must never take advantage of other people's misfortunes to benefit oneself. To do so is the spirit of evil, whereas the spirit of good will is to treat others as one would want to be treated.

If the Israelites are told not to lend to their poor countrymen at interest, they might have decided it was beneficial not to lend to their poor countrymen at all. However, they were commanded to do so. "But thou shalt open thine hand wide unto him, and shalt surely lend him sufficient for his need, in that which he wanteth." (*Deut.* 15:8) A warning is added here: "Beware that there be not a thought in thy wicked heart, saying, 'The seventh year, the year of release, is at hand'. and thine eye be evil against thy poor brother." That is, don't hold back in your lending, thinking that the debt may have to be forgiven, before the debtor can repay it. All outstanding debts were to be forgiven every seven years – the 'sabbath year,' or year of 'release'.

These charitable laws applied to the poor – "For the poor shall never cease out of the land" – but one may suppose it was all right for usurers to lend to foreigners, or to their wealthy countrymen, at whatever interest be gotten, and this seems to be how the law was used. In fact, trade with gentile nations was encouraged, as a way of strengthening Israel. But the Israelites were to be the creditors, not could the debtors. "Thou shalt lend unto many nations, but thou shalt not borrow; and thou shalt reign over many nations, but they shall not reign over thee." (*Deut.* 15:6) Obviously, power lies with the lender, not with the borrower. But if the Israelites disobey god, the tables will turn, and their economy will be cursed: "The stranger that is within thee shall get up above thee very high; and thou shalt come down very low. He shall lend to thee, and thou shalt not lend to him: he shall be the head, and thou shalt be the tail." (*Deut.* 28:44)

The religious laws of charitable lending are reinforced in the moral teachings of Jewish scripture as well. In *Proverbs*: "He that hath pity upon the poor lendeth unto the Lord." (*Prov.* 19:17) And in the *Psalms* of David: "The steps of a good man are ordered by the Lord... He is ever merciful, and lendeth." (*Ps.* 37:23, 26) It is interesting to note that David was sympathetic with the poor from whom he derived, since it is said he counted debtors among his following. "And every one that was in distress, and every one that was in debt, and everyone that was discontented, gathered themselves unto him; and he became a captain over them." (1 *Sam.* 22:2)

Yet despite these encouragements of generosity, it was (and is) always hard to induce money lenders to moderate their ways with a sense of social responsibility. Not surprisingly, we find stories of abuse in the time of the kings, and after the exile, and throughout the books of prophets up to the last. One story, set in the time of Elisha tells of the harshness of a debt against a poor woman, the generosity of her neighbors, and the good outcome for those who obey the divine order. The wife of one of the 'sons of the prophets' (a member of one of a number of prophetic guilds)[43] was widowed and in jeopardy of having her two sons sold as bondsmen to the creditor. She had nothing valuable in the house to sell, except a cruse of olive oil. Elisha, the head of the prophet's guild, told her to borrow empty containers – "borrow not a few" – from her neighbors. When she and her sons began filling the empty vessels from the small pot, miraculously the oil continued flowing until the last container was full. Elisha instructed her to sell the oil to pay the debt, and keep the rest for her own needs. (2 *Kings* 4: 1 – 7)

At the time of the "second exile" to Babylon, Nehemiah, a respected Jew at the court of the Persian king Ataxerxes, was sent to be governor of Jerusalem, and supervise its rebuilding in the late 5th century. He organized the reconstruction, and the defense of the city against enemies. And by his honorable example and authority, he dissuaded his fellow upper-class Jews from taking advantage of their poor countrymen in and around the city, who were forced into debt by conditions of drought and heavy taxation.

> It is not good that ye do: ought ye not to walk in the fear of our God because of the reproach of the heathen our enemies? I likewise, and my brethren, and my servants, might exact of them money and corn: I pray you, let us leave off this usury. Restore, I pray you, to them, even this day, their lands, their vineyards, their oliveyards, and their houses, also the hundredth part[44] of the money, and of the corn, the wine, and the oil, that ye exact of them. (*Neh.* 5:10,11)

The major theme of these scriptural warnings and prohibitions about lending and indebtedness is this: those whom God has blessed should be grateful for his kindness, and feel sympathy for those in need. Especially is it evil to take advantage of the poor and needy by lending to them at interest. This same moral/ religious attitude was carried into the teachings of Jesus, but with two major additions. First, whereas Jews seemed to limit their rules to relations with their Jewish brothers, Jesus made these rules apply universally to all humans as 'brothers' (and sisters as well). Secondly, Jesus emphasized that forgiveness of debts should apply to all social debts, whether material or mental. In Christian scriptures, the word 'debts' is synonymous with any harm or trespass. So, the 'Lord's Prayer,' which Jesus taught to his followers, includes this plea to the heavenly Father:

> And forgive us our debts, as we forgive our debtors ... For if you forgive men their trespasses, your heavenly Father will also forgive you: But if ye forgive not men their trespasses, neither will your Father forgive your trespasses. (*Matt.* 6:12, 14 & 15)

> And forgive us our sins; for we also forgive every one that is indebted to us. (*Luke* 11:4)

We see in these Gospel texts that 'debt,' 'sin' and 'trespass' are used synonymously. In *Matthew*, 'debt' (Greek *opheilo*) and 'trespass' (*paraptoma*) are used interchangeably, while Luke uses 'sin' (*hamartia*) in the place where *Matthew* uses 'debt' (*opheilo*).[45] These Gospel writers are using Greek to interpret Jesus' words, which were spoken in Aramaic, a dialect of Hebrew. Modern Biblical scholarship seems to agree that both *Matthew* (who wrote for a Jewish audience) and *Luke* (who wrote for an international audience, and also authored the book of Acts) were written later than *Mark*, and used the latter as a source. It is thought that *Mark* was written for non-Jewish followers of Jesus, possibly in Syria, around 70 CE (the year that Rome conquered Jerusalem), while *Matthew* and *Luke* were written between 75 CE and 100 CE. In any case, Greek was the written language of the Eastern Mediterranean, and all four Gospels were first written in it.[46]

God is the ultimate creditor

The debt to God, which he is asked to forgive, can't possibly be monetary. We see above that forgiveness of debt is the moral ideal to be sought, and by extension, forgiveness of all trespasses. This is diametrically opposed to the spirit of payback, or vengeance. In fact Jesus suggests that his followers should replace the traditional 'law of retaliation' - an 'eye for an eye' - with the attitude of 'turning the other cheek.' (*Matt.* 5: 39-41) In my view, this doesn't mean that just punishment is forbidden for followers of Christ, but that the spirit of love should replace the spirit of 'getting even,' which so easily enters into traditional justice systems, and which typically is accompanied by personal feelings of hatred.

The idea that if we don't forgive our debtors, God will not forgive our debts to him is problematic, though. One would think that a loving God's forgiveness would be unconditional. In fact, Jesus tells his followers to forgive "seventy times seven"[47] (*Matt.* 18:22) – i.e. without limit, which is the ideal. One should expect that God can and does meet that perfect standard; and in fact Jesus also says that God does forgive all sins. (*Matt.* 12:31; *Mark* 3:28) Strangely, it seems there is one exception, namely the so-called 'unpardonable sin'. "But he that shall blaspheme against the Holy Spirit hath never forgiveness, but is in danger of eternal damnation." (*Mark* 3:29) Does this mean there are limits to God's good will towards humans? No. The point is that despite God's limitless forgiveness, humans can and do reject the Holy Spirit (God), when they reject the spirit of forgiveness and love; and this is equivalent to the rejection of happiness. God can do nothing about that, without violating human choice which is requisite to happiness.

The Ten Commandments and debt

The Ten Commandments, given to the Children of Israel through Moses at Mount Sinai, suggest indebtedness, in both their form and their content. In terms of form, they were given in 'two tables' or 'tablets.' (Deut. 4: 13) This was the traditional way in which a ruler would give law - one copy kept by the king, and one given to the vassal under him. It was also the format for a debt contract.[48] Another way of interpreting 'two tables' is by the division of topics in the Law - one part being obligations to God, and the other being obligations to other humans. Whichever interpretation we choose, the Ten Commandments include a moral view of debt, and its social significance.[49]

In terms of subject matter, one is again reminded that God is the great Creditor, and humans owe him obedience in every detail, and in turn should forgive their debtors. All of this is symbolically akin to the laws about money debt and forgiveness. The Decalogue reminds the hearer that "I am the Lord thy God, who brought thee out of the house of bondage." Humans are in debt to their liberator. And all the subsequent commandments have an overtone of indebtedness. Even the language about coveting is oriented to the proscription against using debt leverage to obtain what one wants, by demanding security in terms of the neighbor's 'house, wife, manservant, maidservant, ox, ass or anything that is thy neighbor's.' The prohibition against adultery is a separate commandment, distinct from 'coveting' a neighbor's wife. In the latter case, she becomes another object of property - among the 'goods' to be demanded in payment of a loan.[50] As one commentator said, a coveting heart is "the root of all sins of word or deed against our neighbor."[51]

Original sins and debt

I said above that the earliest direct reference to debt I could find is the prohibition in *Exodus* (*Ex* 22:20) against lending to the poor at interest. However, I think it can be argued that indebtedness to God is implied in the *Genesis* story of Cain and Able, the children of Adam and Eve, who represent the beginnings of farming culture (and so civilization). They were both obliged, as their culture expected, to bring offerings to God from the fruits of their labors, and both did so. This was a debt to God that they had to pay.

> And in the process of time it came to pass, that Cain brought of the fruit of the ground an offering unto the Lord.
> And Abel, he also brought of the firstlings of his flock and of the fat thereof. And the Lord had respect unto Abel and to his offering;
> But unto Cain and to his offering he had not respect. And Cain was very wroth, and his countenance fell.
> And the Lord said unto Cain, Why art thou wroth? And why is thy countenance fallen?
> If thou doest well, shalt thou not be accepted? and if thou doest not well, sin lieth at the door. (*Gen.* 4:3-7)

The offerings made to God here are typical of cultures close to nature, where the success or failure of crops and herds is believed to depend on pleasing the higher powers, rather than on science. An offering might then be either to pay a debt of gratitude for blessings already received, or as an inducement – a kind of reversal of indebtedness – to ensure that the gods will continue to give blessings. The reason Cain's offering was not accepted is that it gave no evidence of real gratitude; it had no indication of being special. Abel's offering, by contrast, came from the "firstlings of the flock," and included extra fat, which is sweet to taste, and burns brightly. In other words, unlike

Abel, Cain was symbolically holding back, and thinking of himself rather than God. It isn't that God accepts one offering in preference to another. It is that the self-centered gift-giver is not guided by good will – "if thou doest well" – but instead is turning away from God; and so he will not find the happy life God intends for him. Once again, the Divine Creditor gives freely, and forgives all debts. The problem is always with the attitudes of the debtor.

Two seemingly inconsistent parables

Jesus tells two parables, which seem inconsistent with what has been said about debt above. The first – "The unforgiving servant" (*Matt.* 18: 23-35) is about a servant of a great King, who owed his lord the staggering sum of 10,000 talents (roughly a million dollars). When it was found the servant could not pay, the King ordered that he should be sold, together with his wife and children and all his property. The servant fell down and "worshipped him, saying, Lord, have patience with me and I will pay all," upon which the King was moved to pity, and relented. Immediately afterward, this servant went to a fellow servant, who owed him 100 pence (about two dollars),[52] and seizing him by the throat, demanded to be paid. The latter begged for more time, but the unforgiving servant would not have mercy, and cast him into debtors' prison. When the King heard of this, he had the unforgiving servant "delivered to the tormentors, till he should pay all that was due to him".

As the King in the parable is owed an unpayable debt, he obviously represents God, to whom all humans are beholden, and to whom they should be grateful. The parable supports Jesus' addition to the Lord's Prayer, discussed above, that if we don't forgive our debtors, neither will the Father forgive our debts to him. But the degree of violence described here – delivering the merciless servant to the torturers, until the debt should be paid – certainly seems to contradict the idea of God's patience, love and forgiveness, illustrated by the first part of the parable. Furthermore, the idea of exacting payment through torture seems foolish; if the evil doer doesn't have the money, torture won't produce it.

A second story, also problematic from my perspective, is the well-known "Parable of the Talents" (*Matt.* 25:14-30). A master who was going abroad put some of his money into the hands of three servants for them to invest, giving one five talents, another two talents, and a third only one talent – "to every man according to his several ability; and straightway took his journey". When he returned, he called his servants to give account of their investments. The first returned ten talents for the original five, and likewise the second returned four for two. But the third servant, who was 'risk averse,' returned only the one talent given him, which he had buried for safe keeping, saying, "I knew thee that thou art a hard man, reaping where thou hast not sown, and gathering where thou hast not strewed; and I was afraid." The master said that the "wicked and slothful servant," knowing his master's hard reputation, should have "put the money to the exchangers, and then at my coming I should have received mine own with usury." He added,

> Take therefore the talent from him, and give it unto him which hath ten talents. For unto him that hath shall be given, and he shall have abundance; but from him that hath not shall be taken away even that which he hath. (*Matt.* 25:29)

The difficulty here is the caricature the parable gives of God. He is a "hard" business man, reaping where he has not sown, which suggests he seeks undeserved and high 'return on investment' (in this case, one hundred percent!). Secondly, his servants are enjoined to invest the money they are lent in money lending enterprises, and return it "with usury," which contradicts the laws previously discussed. Third, the parable suggests that God is unfair, rewarding those who are successful with further benefits, and taking away from the less fortunate even the little they have. And finally, instead of forgiving the servant who was afraid of his master, God casts the "unprofitable" servant into "outer darkness." (*Matt.* 25: 30) At least the master in this case did not deliver the unprofitable servant to the tormentors to pay off his debt, as did the King of the previous parable.

This can't possibly be a picture of the loving Father of whom Jesus speaks. It is more like the holy terror of *Exodus*, who 'hardened the heart' of Pharaoh, and then brought plagues on all the Egyptians because of their recalcitrant ruler. (*Ex.* 7:3,4) But what does it mean? People have long recognized that this parable is about personal talents, rather than money – talents which are God given and should not be wasted.[53] And it is in this context that the master must be seen. It is, however, still a view of the divine creditor. The debts here are not about the money that is owed by one's Jewish neighbor, which should be forgiven; nor is it about the sins of one's neighbor, which Christians believe should also be forgiven; it is about the debt to God that must be paid. How does one pay back his debt to that Master? He does this by paying his debt to his fellow humans. As Jesus goes on to say, adding to the parable of the talents:

> Then shall the righteous answer him saying, Lord, when saw we thee an hungered, and fed thee, or thirsty, and gave thee drink? When saw we thee a stranger, and took thee in? or naked, and clothed thee? Or when saw we thee sick, or in prison, and came unto thee? And the King shall answer and say unto them, Verily I say unto you, inasmuch as ye have done it unto one of the least of these brethren, ye have done it unto me. (*Matt.* 25:37-40)

Debts to God, then, can only be paid by benefitting ones neighbor. The wicked and slothful servant ignored his debt to God. Refusing to serve his neighbor, except insofar as it would benefit himself, he buried his one talent (it matters not whether it was one or many), in the tomb of self-interest, where happiness can't be found. I think that the saying "For unto every one that hath shall be given, and he will have abundance, but from him that hath not shall be taken away even that which he hath" is a description of the prospects for limitless development and happiness of those who try to serve their neighbors, and the diminishment and frustration of those who don't. Again, God loves all people equally and boundlessly, without conditions. Our material welfare and health may often be out of our hands, but our spiritual welfare and happiness depend on our choices. This is implied in all the texts we have been examining.

Second thoughts on scripture: Girard and Swedenborg

So far in this chapter, I have summarized some scriptural principles with respect to debt and debt forgiveness (and by extension, forgiveness of all offenses). Here I will briefly introduce the thoughts of two men of science – one living now, and the other from the 18th century – about deeper ways to 'read' Biblical scripture generally: Rene Girard, and Emanuel Swedenborg. Then I'll use their ideas to examine briefly the symbolism of wealth and poverty in other scriptural examples.

Rene Girard

Rene Girard was born in France, in 1923, but he has spent most of his life teaching in the United States – primarily at Stanford University. He is one of forty so-called "*immortels*" – current members of the venerable *Academie* Francaise – elected in 2005 as a renowned scholar of anthropology, literary criticism, history, philosophy and religious mythology. He is also a religious believer, which puts him outside the mainstream of American social scientists and academics, and may explain why his research and theories are not more widely known.

Girard's main studies focus on the idea that all primal societies were born out of a state of chaotic competition that resulted from "mimetic desire" – i.e. from people's natural tendency to *want what others want* - which leads to conflict and violence. When this conflict becomes violent enough, people will inevitably and spontaneously seize on someone to blame for their disorder – a scapegoat – whom they will kill or drive away. That is the nature of primitive thinking, or group psychology of the sort that Freud and others have analyzed.[54]

Paradoxically, the very unity the primal group feels in focusing on one scapegoat as the 'source of all their troubles' brings order back into the group. So after ridding themselves of the innocent victim, they view her or him as both the source of all their troubles and the bringer of order and peace. In other words, they attribute to her, or him, divine powers for both evil and good; she must have been a god! As a result, the group constructs a mythical and ritual 'explanation' of themselves – a *religion* – centering on the destructive/ beneficial power of their scapegoat/ savior; and they continue to use the story and its ritual reenactment to maintain group order into the future. The myth always hides the fact that the group killed an innocent scapegoat; it wouldn't be good or even possible to kill their god. Girard shows, in many, many examples of myths from around the world, how this truth-concealing mechanism can be seen in the indirect, symbolic language of the myths.[55]

All primal religions (and the societies they structure) began thus in violence. This is true of the 'Abrahamic' religions too. But Girard shows that biblical religions differ in one basic, all- important way, from other 'mythic' religions: Biblical scriptures *don't hide the act of scapegoating*. The innocence of the victims is always seen clearly in dozens of examples throughout the Scriptures, leading up to the greatest scapegoat – Jesus – and the violence is never excused. In Girard's interpretation then, *forgiveness* is the message throughout the Abrahamic scriptures, from beginning to end. That is, we must find a non-violent way of bringing order to society, or we will destroy ourselves and the world in the name of righteousness. This destructive potential of mimetic rivalry is the prediction of the various apocalyptic parts of Jewish and Christian scripture.

The message of God's kingdom as a kingdom of peace is there from the beginning, but it doesn't show clearly on the surface. It becomes clearer and clearer, however, in the progressive writing of the Jewish testament, and is most obvious in the Christian testament. Nevertheless, people today continue to miss the message, obviously. (Girard doesn't know to what degree this kind of message is also present in Islamic scriptures, because he has not been able to study the *Qur'an* enough to judge.)

Emanuel Swedenborg

Emanuel Swedenborg (1688 – 1772) spent his life in Sweden, but traveled to other parts of Europe, including stays in Italy, Holland and England. He was a well-respected member of the Swedish house of nobles, the parliament, and the Royal Academy of Sciences in Sweden. As an engineer and inventor, he worked for the royal government as inspector in the Board of Mines, even while pursuing his private studies in philosophy, science and religion.[56] Swedenborg lived in the 'Age of Science.' He was born a year after Newton first published his theory of the laws of motion. Like many other Enlightenment thinkers, Swedenborg retained his religious (or spiritual) beliefs even while emphasizing the role of reason, science and the value of experience in truth-seeking. For him religion was not a matter of orthodoxy, and it certainly wasn't the kind of emotional fundamentalism popular today (especially in America), which is a reaction to scientific theories,[57] and which contemporary scientists usually reject outright.

Swedenborg believed that truth has objective existence, which is grounded in ultimate reality (The Divine). Truth can be discovered in all realms of thought – scientific, aesthetic, moral and spiritual – by a rational, good-willed and modest seeker. But at the highest level, it needs revelation. In looking at Biblical scripture, Swedenborg's insight was this: Whatever ideas lie on the surface of the original texts, whether they are true, false, or ambiguous, there is always an interior and an innermost level of truth in every genuine revelation (for example, in "Moses and the prophets" as Jesus called the Jewish testament). This higher or inner truth involves human spiritual life, and is true for all time and every person, regardless of historic or cultural changes.

Needless to say, finding this 'inner truth' of Scripture requires interpretation; it involves symbolism, and poetic or "correspondential" meanings, and providential guidance. Swedenborg illustrates this approach in his detailed analysis of *Genesis* and *Exodus* – which was published in ten Latin volumes from 1749 to 1756 - and shows how the same principles apply to the whole of Jewish and Christian scriptures, by taking copious examples from *Genesis* through *Revelations*. Following these interpretative approaches of Girard and Swedenborg, I will analyze a few more biblical references to money and poverty, and suggest their deeper or broader implications.

Symbolism of rich and poor in Biblical scripture

It is often possible to find a deep meaning in Biblical language by thinking metaphorically about the literal meaning. That is to say, consider the way in which a literal term operates in the world of everyday experience, and then look for an analogy in the mental realm. For instance, the word "light" occurs throughout Scripture, as well as the various sources of light (e.g. sun, star, morning, moon, lightning and lamp). No one has trouble seeing this as an analogy to "truth" in its various forms; indeed, light symbolism is in every culture's literature. But there are other Biblical terms which in context can also direct our thinking towards truth and its functions in the mental or spiritual realm (e.g. a stone, a pearl, rock, seed, a two-edged sword, water, and wine); but the one I want to emphasize here is "riches" or "wealth" or "money." The particular meanings depend on the context, and on the kind of truth symbolized.

"Blessed are the poor in spirit"

It seems very strange to speak of poverty of any kind as a "blessing," or even as a promise of blessing. What does it mean to be "poor in spirit"? To understand this, we need to look at earthly or material poverty, and similarly, we need to look at the deeper meaning of riches, wealth and money to understand their metaphorical use in scriptural texts. Simply put, poverty is the condition that keeps a person from accomplishing the goals she or he intends or desires. So riches are the material means for attaining the material ends that a person seeks.

To what degree a person feels deprived and limited by poverty is subjective, of course. Buddhist literature is full of examples that encourage people to 'let go' of such matters, and so liberate themselves mentally. But there is no doubt that the material means for accomplishing material goals are real. I can't buy a house without money, whether or not I may be able to avoid suffering about it. And as a friend pointed out, somewhat cynically, even Buddha and his followers had lands to work, and gifts from supporters, and in a pinch, monks always had their begging bowls. Quite simply, Biblical 'riches' are truth – especially the truth about what is good and important and should be sought out. It is the truth that guides people, that gives them the right priorities, that puts childish illusions into perspective, and that helps everyone to know what happiness is and how to find it.

Specifically, spiritual riches symbolize the truth of revelation – i.e. the Word, as it is called – although what 'the Word' refers to is itself also a matter of interpretation. In a Biblical context, then, poor people (the 'poor in spirit') are those who lack this spiritual wealth.

The poor in spirit are those who lack these spiritual means, and are aware of the fact, and wish to change it. They desire spiritual knowledge and want to lead good lives. It is this awareness and this desire that will lead them to accept the truth when it is offered. Truth exists in various 'realms' – in mathematics, in science, in practical skills, in moral matters, and in the 'life of the spirit.' In every case, truth is what is needed to fulfill the goal; truth is the money or treasure. There are natural needs and spiritual needs. They should be prioritized.

Biblical texts harp on this idea. David says, "I rejoice at your word as one who finds great treasure." (*Ps.* 119: 162) Jesus says, "Lay not up for yourselves treasures on earth, where moth and dust destroy, and thieves break in and steal; but lay up for yourselves treasures in heaven." (*Matt.* 6: 19,20)

The rich young ruler

Of course, people can abuse riches too. They can horde money and put it to no use; or waste it; or spend it conspicuously to cause envy, or to feel superior; or use it to control and harm others. Subjectively, riches can be sought for the wrong reasons; objectively riches can be put to the wrong uses. And so the term 'riches' can be a metaphor even for the opposite of truth; it can mean falsity. Instead of the guidance of the 'good word,' riches can be "deceitful." (*Micah* 6: 12; and *Matt.* 13: 22) Riches can suffocate the truth, just as cares of the world get in the way of following its guidance. This is developed in the Parable of the Sower. (*Matt.* 13: 22)

Jesus has an interesting discussion with his disciples about the dangers of wealth, in *Mark*, which scholars suggest is the first Gospel, to which later 'evangelists' referred. I mention this because Mark may give the truest account of what Jesus actually said. The context here is that Jesus was healing people and teaching by parables, and apparently gained a big following. A "rich young ruler" came to Jesus, knelt in honor to him, and asked "Good Teacher, what shall I do that I may inherit eternal life?" (*Mark* 10: 17) This man seems well motivated, but the Teacher rebuked him nevertheless:

"Why do you call me good? No one is good but One, that is God. You know the commandments: 'Do not commit adultery,' 'Do not murder,' 'Do not steal,' 'Do not defraud,' 'Honor your father and your mother.' And he answered and said to him, "Teacher, all these I have observed from my youth."

Then Jesus, looking at him, loved him, and said to him "One thing you lack: Go your way, sell whatever you have and give to the poor, and you will have treasure in heaven; and come, take up the cross, and follow me." But he was sad at this word, and went away grieved, for he had great possessions. (*Mark* 10: 18-22)

The surface lesson of this story is apparent; the deeper message is not. I think the deeper message holds up better, and is not so extreme; but first the surface message. Jesus seems to be saying that the way to 'eternal life' requires giving all one's material wealth to the poor, and 'taking up the cross' to follow him (even after he is no longer in the world). Hearing this, Peter, in his youthful naivety enthusiastically says 'Look at us; we've given up everything and followed you,' to which Jesus answers that no one who has left house or brothers or sisters or father or mother or wife or children or lands "for my sake and the gospel's," will fail to get all these things back again a hundredfold "now in this time … with persecutions – and in the age to come, eternal life." (*Mark* 10: 28-30) He promises a very good 'return on investment' indeed, *even in this world* (though it may be accompanied by 'persecutions'), as well as in the age to come (presumably 'heaven', whatever that intends.) Could this be true literally? And is material wealth truly a barrier to heaven or happiness?

Look again at the rich young man. What were his faults? Why was he rebuked, and what was the second chance he didn't take? First, what was wrong with calling Jesus "Good Master"? It was that God is the ultimate good – the source of goods of all sorts – and should be put first in priority of one's values. It seems the young 'ruler' had some sort of authority in the Jewish community; perhaps he was part of the political elite at a time of tension with the Roman overlords. In addition, he was looking for eternal life – certainly a valuable goal. His goodness, however, consists of conformity to the rules of the *Decalogue* – the Ten Commandments.

Every culture in the world has one version or another of these basic rules, not, I think, because God gave them, but because they bring order to society. Most people follow them as a matter of course, if they are raised in a decent social environment. An educated person easily sees that it's more beneficial to keep the rules than to break them, because we all understand it will work to our favor, especially in a small, traditional society, where everyone knows his neighbor's business. This smart conformity is called 'enlightened self-interest.' Although our actions may not be harmful to others, or may even benefit others, the motives for them are selfish nonetheless, and do not count in our spiritual growth. Unfortunately, in a large, urban, anonymous society like our own, many of us do break these rules (commandments) when it seems we can do so with impunity. We should do the 'right thing' because it is right, and not because it serves us well.

Jesus told the young ruler that "the one thing you lack" could be corrected by selling his possessions and by giving to the poor; and of course, when he freed himself from his social status, he could also 'take up his cross,' and follow Jesus. What was 'lacking' to the young man was the right motive. He needed 'spiritual poverty,' or the correct view of what is valuable – the correct understanding of good – and a life according to that view. This "one thing" is a big thing indeed, not in the sense of being difficult (although it is), but in the sense of being all important. As the Master comments to his disciples, "How hard it is for those who have riches to enter the kingdom of God." (*Mark* 10: 23) He immediately repeats himself: "Children, how hard it is for those who trust in riches to enter the kingdom of God." (*Mark* 10: 24) Note the slight but all significant difference – "those who *have* riches" and "those who *trust in* riches" – and this is what makes the rich young man be sad, and why he goes away grieved. He trusts his riches.

Children and many adults think their natural desires are good, and should be gratified. They have a false sense of riches. Their self-interest may make them reject the truth which is offered, by those with wisdom and revelation, and replace it with their material idea of good. This is natural and understandable. But the 'rich man' is one who knows what is right and good - he has the Word - but he doesn't care about it, or perverts the truth and uses it to his private advantage. In Biblical scripture, the most important truth is not about science or worldly knowledge, although that is good and useful; rather it is that which leads to a spiritual life, to concern for others' welfare as well as one's own, and to real happiness. Not only does a person need to know that truth; she needs to live it, and show it to others.

Jesus is particularly critical of people who have the truth and don't share it, or use it for good purpose; instead, they puff themselves up for being superior to others who are outside the inner circle. There are many cases where he faults empty orthodoxy. "You think you are rich, but you are poor," (*Rev.* 3:17) while he encourages those who feel ignorant, but are searching for spiritual answers. (*Rev.* 2: 9) These are the 'poor in spirit.' These long for the truth, and rejoice when they find it. Nor does the truth need to be complex; the details of the many laws of Jewish orthodoxy may be beneficial (although on the surface, I don't think so), but the core is what gives them value – certainly not their memorization or much repetition. If there is a single doctrine that illuminates all the rest of "the law and the prophets" it is this: Love God and love your neighbor as yourself. (*Matt.* 22: 37 – 40 and *Deut.* 6:5, 10:12; 30:6.) This makes sense of life and leads to happiness. It is the "pearl of great price," which out-values all other riches (*Matt.* 13: 46), to which all other knowledge can be of service.

The crumbs which fall from the master's table

By contrast to this rich young man, we have the story of a Canaanite woman's exchange with Jesus. She was not in the Jewish community. She was an outsider, because she was not privy to the "law and the prophets" given to Abraham and his heirs. She didn't have 'the Word,' and because of this, she would have been scorned by the orthodox establishment. In Jewish terms, she was a 'gentile' – a member of 'the nations.' Her story is told directly after Jesus left the area around the Sea of Galilee, and went north to work near Tyre. He had chastised his orthodox critics who came from Jerusalem to observe his activities, calling them hypocrites and comparing them to those whom Isaiah, long before, had accused of honoring God "with their lips, but their heart is far from me. And in vain they worship me, teaching as doctrines the commandments of men." (*Matt.* 15: 9; Is 29:13)

The Canaanite woman came to Jesus, calling out for him to heal her demon-possessed daughter, but he seemed to ignore her loud crying. Yet when the disciples asked him to send her away, he quieted them, saying "I was not sent except to the lost sheep of the house of Israel." She was one of those lost sheep, being beyond the pale – a Northerner, or 'hick'. When she asked again for help, he apparently insulted her, saying "It is not good to take the children's bread and throw it to the little dogs." (*Matt.* 15:26) She was not at all deterred, and answered "True, Lord, yet even the little dogs eat of the crumbs which fall from their master's table." At this show of faith, the Master granted her wish.

Lazarus and the rich man

It is curious that the Canaanite woman referred to 'dogs eating the crumbs which fall from a master's table,' because the same idea is found in the gospel of *Matthew*, in the parable of Lazarus and the rich man. Perhaps it was a common metaphor; it surely gives a vivid picture. That's why I chose it as the cover illustration for this essay.

> Now there was a certain rich man who was clothed in purple and fared sumptuously every day. But there was a certain beggar named Lazarus, full of sores, who was laid at his gate, desiring to be fed with the crumbs which fell from the rich man's table. Moreover, the dogs came and licked his sores. (*Luke* 16:19-21)

Both the rich man and Lazarus died, and in the after-life one was in hades, while the other was in Abraham's bosom. The rich man, in torment, called out to Abraham to send Lazarus to 'dip the tip of his finger in water, and cool my tongue.' Abraham explained that each had received his just reward, and besides, a "great gulf" separated the two realms. In a paradoxical display of altruism, the rich man asked that Abraham send Lazarus to his house, where five errant brothers still lived, "that he may testify to them, lest they also come to this place of torment." Abraham answered that they should listen to Moses and the prophets. The rich man insisted that "if one goes to them from the dead, they will repent;" but Abraham retorted, "If they do not hear Moses and the prophets, neither will they be persuaded though one rise from the dead." (*Luke* 16: 19-31)

As said before, "Moses and the prophets" or "the law and the prophets" is short-hand for the whole of revelation; it is '*Dabar YHWH*' (the 'Word of God'). Water is another symbol for truth. It can (or could have) slaked the tormented rich man's thirst, if he had recognized its value – i.e. if he had realized his spiritual poverty, but symbolically he had the opposite mindset. His attitude towards truth was to use it for his own purposes, or to reject it. The parable also seems to be saying that accepting the truth (i.e. believing in the Word) doesn't depend on miracles. Emotional persuasion is not belief. Neither does it depend on rational 'proof.' In fact, as Kierkegaard pointed out in the 19th century, belief doesn't *depend* on anything. It is a matter of free choice; otherwise it wouldn't be ours.[58] But the point for our discussion here is that the choice is between 'riches' in the material sense, and 'riches' in the spiritual sense. Between the two, a 'great gulf is fixed.' It is up to each person to decide which has priority, and the consequences follow. The choice is made in this life; not in another.

Man shall not live by bread alone

"Crumbs" bring to mind bread. We often say we have to have money, to earn our "bread". Clearly, both money and the bread which it buys represent basic necessities – the needs or demands of worldly life. The Lord's Prayer asks God to "Give us this day our daily bread". It goes on to say, "and forgive us our debts as we forgive our debtors". The latter text signifies that we need to see God as the ultimate creditor, to whom everyone is indebted, as was discussed in the previous section. Daily bread is the food that sustains us. Symbolically, it is spiritual food that goes far beyond our material needs. Although most of us wish a diet that is better than bread and water, we all recognize that these are basic, without which we would die. God provides what truly sustains us, regardless of the extravagance of our worldly tastes, or our sense of independence. We are also reminded that what God provides is everything necessary and sufficient for spiritual sustenance – and for lasting happiness. No need to starve.

In their difficult wanderings in the wilderness, God provided 'manna' miraculously to sustain the Israelites. It is possible that the word 'manna' derives from the question 'What is it?' Apparently it was some sort of plant substance that could be ground into flour, with which the people were unfamiliar. In any case, it became tiresome, and the Israelites complained because they didn't have meat. Manna had to be gathered daily. It couldn't be horded, or else it "bred worms and stank". But it provided 'daily bread' for the children of Israel. The experience taught them to be grateful to God, and to raise their thoughts above worldly success to the attainment of spiritual riches, which are found in God's word; the latter leads not just to a full belly, but to spiritual fulfillment and happiness. This is how Moses put it:

So he humbled you, allowed you to hunger, and fed you with manna which you did not know nor did your fathers know that He might make you to know that man shall not live by bread alone; but man lives by every word that proceeds from the mouth of the Lord. (*Deut.* 8: 3)

This text suggests that riches of any sort – even if only in the form of the small amount of food needed to eke out a daily existence – is provided through some kind of truth or knowledge. In other words, 'bread,' like 'riches,' represents truth, symbolically and existentially. From a Biblical perspective, all things ultimately are traceable to the divine truth, or 'the Word.'

For the poor will never cease from the land

The Biblical principles summarized here, about riches, poverty (and relatedly, about debt and social responsibility), have been known for at least four thousand years. They were true in the time of Abraham and Moses, in the time of the prophets, in the time of Jesus, and I think they are true today; and a believer would say they will always be true. But will poverty disappear as societies develop? The Jewish and Christian revelators say no. Moses says "For the poor will never cease from the land; therefore I command you, saying, You shall open your hand wide to your brother, to the poor and your needy, in your land." (*Deut.* 15:11) And Jesus says the same, but with an addition. "For you have the poor with you always, and whenever you wish you may do them good; but me you do not have always." (*Mark* 14:7; *Matt.* 26:11; *John* 12:8)

The interesting difference here is that Jesus points out he will not always be with his disciples; yet in another place, he says "I am with you always, even to the end of the age." (*Matt.* 28:20) The two statements are interconnected because of events that were unfolding quickly. The context of the first instance is that a woman had poured expensive ointment on Jesus' feet, and his disciples complained that it was a waste of something precious which could have been sold for money to support the poor. Jesus said to leave her alone, because she was doing it 'for a memorial' in anticipation of his death which he had predicted, and which was imminent. The second instance was shortly after his death, when he appeared to the disciples, sent them out to preach the 'good news,' and promised his continued support.

Analyzing the claim that "*the poor will never cease from the land*" shows it to be a continuation, and even a summary of the other themes we've examined in this section, as well as the more general Biblical principles about money and debt discussed in the previous section. The disciples were eager to help the poor – which is certainly in keeping with Jesus' message. What they failed to see was that Jesus himself *is* the "riches" which can satisfy the needs of the poor. It is believed not only that Jesus had access to the divine truth, or 'the Word; he is the *embodiment* of that Word or truth. John, for instance, says "In the beginning was the Word, and the Word was with God, and the Word was God …. And the Word became flesh, and dwelt among us." (*John* 1:1; 1:14) John is the 'deepest' of the gospel writers. He understood well the metaphysics and the mystery of Scripture. His ideas about the interconnections of the divine source, its material manifestation and mankind are similar to those of South Asian religions, and appeal to philosophical, rational minds.

But will there always be poor people? If we hold to the 'inner meaning' of poverty, the answer is yes, whether or not progressive societies may one day overcome the abject material deprivations that still exist around the world. There will always be the spiritually poor, because poverty of spirit is ignorance – especially ignorance of what is important, and how best to find happiness. Every life begins in ignorance; everyone must learn the truth. Although no one wants to be poor, materially or spiritually, this deeper Biblical viewpoint suggests that all people must become 'poor in spirit' by recognizing their need for truly satisfying riches, knowing the unlimited source of those riches, and by seeing that these riches are freely offered for the 'blessing' of anyone who will ask.

Chapter Five

Debt, Wealth and Oligarchy

The rich get richer and the poor get poorer

Chapter 4 above examined religious and moral principles according to which debt relations and wealth should be ordered. In this and the following chapter, we'll look at questions of control over the national economy. This is partly an analysis of influences that are presently dominant, and partly some views about which influences ought to be dominant, both in the economy as a whole, and in the debt relations among individuals at the personal level. Chapter 5 will analyze the rather dark (some would say cynical) view that oligarchs determine the general shape and outcomes of the economy for their own benefit, to the detriment of the society at large. Chapter 6 will summarize some problems and some solutions about indebtedness and the 'public good' in our secular democratic society. We should keep in mind that theories must be read with an eye on practicalities and on experience, to avoid being dogmatic and disconnected from reality. We should remember too that ideas and behavior, of individuals and of groups, involve degrees of freedom and unpredictability, for good and ill.

In a 1986 interview, Gore Vidal commented about the United States under the administration of Ronald Reagan: "The genius of our system is that ordinary people go out and vote against their interests. The way our ruling class keeps out of sight is one of the greatest stunts in the political history of any country."[59] In my opinion, this statement summarizes clearly the steady development of oligarchy and its influence in America over the past forty years. For a scholarly history of the subject, and an overview of its form and influence in the US today, I recommend Jeffrey Winters' *Oligarchy*.[60] In keeping with an earlier promise, I'll try to present my views objectively. However, I don't think there can be much rational argument against the idea that oligarchy exists in the US; that its power has increased greatly over the past forty years; and that its influence on the public good is generally negative.

The term 'oligarchy' comes from Greek *oligarkhia*, rooted in oligos ('few') and *arkhein* ('to rule') – i.e. rule by the few. Aristotle used the term to describe one of the deviant forms of constitution, parallel to 'aristocracy' which he thought more just.[61] Given that historically the ruling few have been the very rich, a better term might be 'plutocracy,' from Greek *ploutokratia*, rooted in *ploutos* ('wealth') and *kratia* ('power') – i.e. power of the wealthy. Both terms are used today, but oligarchy is more common, so I'll keep that.

Winters describes four basic forms of oligarchy that have existed around the world, over time. All of them share the primary goal of protecting their wealth. The differences come from how this is accomplished. "Warring oligarchy" occurs when warlords compete for wealth by violence, and seek to enlarge their holdings by dominating other warlords' domains. This happened, for example, in Medieval Europe under regional monarchs, and with the feuding families of 19th century American Appalachia.[62]

"Ruling oligarchy" occurs when oligarchs take political control collectively, as happened in Greece and Rome and in the city states of late medieval Italy, like Venice and Florence. Winters uses the uncomfortable term "sultanistic oligarchy" for a third type. This involves a ruler – a sultan such as Marcos in the Philippines, and Suharto in Indonesia – who permits oligarchs to keep and advance their wealth only to the degree that they collaborate with the dictator. The fourth type - "civil oligarchy"- occurs when a civil society, such as the U.S. today, makes laws that protect the wealth of oligarchs. And their wealth provides almost unlimited means to accomplish this, literally at the expense of, and often to the detriment of the country at large.

Wealth distribution trends/ Changes in wealth inequality

The table and two 'pie' graphs that follow show the pattern of wealth distribution in the U.S. over the past twenty-five to thirty years, as well as how 'net worth' and 'financial wealth' compare. It has changed slowly to the disadvantage of the poor.[63]

Financial (non-home) Wealth

	Top 1 %	Next 19 %	Bottom 80 %
1983	42.9%	48.4%	8.7%
1989	46.9$	46.5%	6.6%
1992	45.6%	46.7%	7.7%
1995	47.2%	45.9%	7.0%
1998	47.3%	43.6%	9.1%
2001	39.7%	51.5%	8.7%

2004	42.2%	50.3%	7.5%
2007	42.7%	50.3%	7.0%
2010	42.1%	53.5%	4.7%

US net worth and financial wealth distribution in 2010

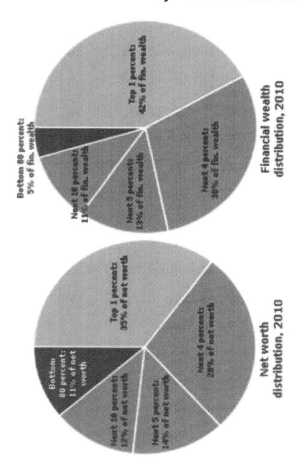

It's noteworthy, but not surprising, that the general public has no idea about income disparities or wealth distribution statistics, especially at the top and the bottom of the scales. The top 20% of the population own over 95% of the wealth; the bottom 20% own 0.3% - a number too small to register on the graphs.[64] It's interesting that financial data about the group of individuals at the very top of the ladder was not even publicly available from government agencies until 2009. Today the IRS gives information about the top 400 persons, whose average income is about $350 million per year.

The following chart shows that CEO pay has increased greatly in the same period, from 1983 to 2007. This disparity is far greater in the U.S. than in any other country, and many people think it is actually harmful to the economy, aside from questions of fairness.[65]

CEO's pay as multiple of average worker's pay, 1960 – 2007

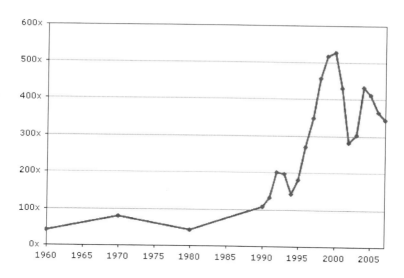

Taken from Domhoff, "Wealth, Income and Power;" original source: "Executive Excess 2008," by Institute for Policy Studies and United for a Fair Economy.

Our fair share

Contrary to popular belief, trends in tax laws similarly favor the wealthy. In fact, taken as whole, the US tax system is "regressive" – i.e. falling more heavily on the poor than on the wealthy. This is increasingly the case during the last thirty years, since Reagan's tax policies took effect. As Warren Buffet, the CEO of Berkshire Hathaway, famously pointed out in 2011, the people in his office with ordinary income pay higher tax rates than he does. He noted that 88 of the top 400 had "no wages at all", although they made a great deal of income through 'capital gains', which are taxed at a lower rate than ordinary income. Buffet suggested raising the rate considerably. Most significantly, he pointed out that many of his rich friends had paid higher taxes in times past, and he was sure that higher rates would not stop them from investing in the future.[66] Of course, not everyone listed in the Forbes 400 (e.g. the Koch brothers) thinks the "Buffet Tax" is a good idea.

In 1889, Andrew Carnegie expressed the obligation he thought men of great wealth have to use their good fortune wisely for the benefit of the public which allowed them to prosper. Rather than pass his wealth to his children, or bequeath it to some public institution after his death, the rich man should oversee the distribution of his money to benefit his community. In "The Gospel of Wealth" Carnegie expressed this belief honorably (if somewhat snobbishly), and followed it in his practice. One wonders if such a philosophy could possibly be hoped for today. Apparently the government thought not, as it amended the Constitution twenty five years later. In his essay, Carnegie enjoined the man of wealth:

> First, to set an example of modest, unostentatious living, shunning display or extravagance; to provide moderately for the legitimate wants of those dependent upon him and after doing so to consider all surplus revenues which come to him simply as trust funds, which he is called upon to administer, and strictly

bound as a matter of duty to administer in the manner which, in his judgment, is best calculated to produce the most beneficial results for the community--the man of wealth thus becoming the mere agent and trustee for his poorer brethren, bringing to their service his superior wisdom, experience and ability to administer, doing for them better than they would or could do for themselves.[67]

Many people criticize the present tax system, mostly negatively, whatever their political orientation. That's the nature of the beast. Joseph Stiglitz recently drew attention to some problems, in a New York Times editorial. The highest tax rate was 70% through the 1970's and 1980's, but in the Reagan presidency it dropped to about 35% and stayed there (until this year). At present the top 1% of the population earns 20% of the national income, and pays 20% of the tax bill, which is a 'flat rate'; Stiglitz thinks it should be 'progressive'. He also notes that there are many 'subsidies' for the wealthy, giving special rates "for vacation homes, racetracks, beer breweries, oil refineries, hedge funds and movie studios". He criticizes the "so-called carried interest," by which some financiers are taxed at lower rates for income they derive from managing private equity funds or hedge funds.[68]

Stiglitz fails to mention other kinds of subsidies for the better off, such as interest on home mortgage loans; special rates for favored industries, like oil drilling; write offs for agribusiness crop losses; patent right extensions for merely 'tweaking' pharmaceutical formulae over and over; low tax rates on capital gains (as Buffet critiqued above); low inheritance taxes (which now can be avoided altogether by setting up estate funds in perpetuity), etc.[69]

Despite these criticisms, questions about what is 'fair,' and what is best for overall economic development, are in the end matters of differences of judgment, which are beyond my ability to evaluate in general. In any case, I think these income tax issues are often a side issue and distraction, for two reasons. First, they frame the argument in terms of class warfare, with one party 'hating the rich' and looking for higher taxes, and the other 'hating the government' and looking for lower taxes. As economist Stephanie Kelton recently put it,

> President Obama told the nation, "We're out of money." All of this is utter nonsense, as readers of this blog know, and it leaves progressives in the weak position of pointing at the 1% and yelling, "Get 'em! They've got all the money!" Want to care for seniors? Tax the 1%. Want safe roads, good schools, investment in alternative energy? Tax the 1%. The problem, of course, is that the 1% tend to fight back …and win! The truth is, we're not broke. The US dollar comes from the US government (not from China, as we're led to believe). The US government is not revenue constrained. It is the Issuer of the currency, not the User of the currency like you and I. It plays by a completely different set of rules, yet it behaves as if it is still bound by the shackles of a gold standard. It behaves irresponsibly when it proposes policies to reduce the deficit when unemployment is high and inflation is low. We're letting millions of Americans suffer because Pete Peterson and his ilk have convinced virtually everyone that we face a fiscal crisis in this country. We live in fear of the Chinese, the Ratings Agencies, the Bond Vigilantes, Indentured Grandchildren, and so on. And this fear is uses by politicians on both sides of the political aisle to sell "sacrifice" to the rest of us. And we keep buying it.[70]

The second reason these income tax rates and special discounts are a side issue is that the tax system works against the people at the lower end of the scale, which in principle are those who most need the society's help. Sales taxes are a greater burden for those whose income is spent mainly on day to day purchases, like food, clothing, transportation, electricity, etc. Rental property taxes are passed along directly to renters. Furthermore, public schooling costs are covered by property taxes, so people in poorer neighborhoods have poor schools as well. Finally, some thinkers argue that 'payroll taxes' which cover social security, Medicare and other government programs, fall more heavily on poorer people, because the wealthier class makes income from sources other than wages. And state and local tax systems are typically 'flat,' so they take a greater fraction of the income of the less well off. All of these ways of paying for government suggest an overall 'regressive' characteristic of public sector funding, for those at the very bottom and the very top. For the middle class, government funding policies may be more 'progressive.' In other words, it appears that there are systemic disadvantages for those already disadvantaged, and systemic advantages to those already advantaged. Even so, all these questions are greatly disputed, regardless of one's perspective about any 'obligation' (or social debt) to one group of citizens or another.

The wealth defense industry

Whether or not one considers the tax system to be unfair, or even bad for the economy, it's clear that there is in place a very effective campaign – increasingly successful in the last thirty to forty years - to protect the wealth of oligarchs from taxation and other threats. Winters shows convincingly how an entire extremely lucrative industry has developed to maintain and increase oligarchic wealth, not to mention a constant publicity campaign to hide, disguise or reinterpret the facts, to make them palatable to the public. This industry consists of prestigious law firms, and their highly paid lawyers; top tier banking and investment advisers; and lobbyists and technical experts whose interests and success lies in their ability to defend their clients' wealth against forces that threaten it – e.g. through governmental laws that tax them directly, or otherwise diminish their sources of wealth.

Some items in the toolbox of wealth defense

There are many ways in which the wealth defense industry can accomplish its (and its clients') goals. They develop with practice, and change according to technical advances, and the political climate of the society where they are employed. I will summarize a few of the more common ones here, taking most of the information from Jeffery Winters' book and sources he uses.

Keep it under the radar

This is probably the first principle for wealth defense, which is implied by Gore Vidal's quote above regarding oligarchy. Not surprisingly, the 'wealth defense industry' tries to keep its activities, and the names of its clients, out of the public lime light. And equally unsurprising, some firms in the industry occasionally lose sight of where their success lies, and begin to market their various wealth-generating and wealth-protecting 'instruments' to a wider public. (It's a bit like 'haute couture' clothing designers of Europe making mass-produced copies for the general market.) The exposure of oligarchic activity may bring public attention, government investigation, and litigation, such as happened in 2003 with a 'scandal' involving KPMG – a firm combining Peat Marwick and Klynveld Goerdeler, of Dutch roots . I put 'scandal' in inverted commas, because the Senate hearings of that case resulted only in some fines of one firm in a huge industry, no penalties of any kind for its oligarchic clients (it being suggested that they were 'led astray' by the firm), and little or no change in the system.[71]

Offshore accounts and corporations

These are among the many techniques which continue to change and develop to serve the wealth defense industry. These 'tax havens' conceal perhaps $15 trillion to $20 trillion from governmental taxation (and more, if one counts Swiss banks as 'off shore' and off shore real estate as part of wealth). Given the difficulty of gathering data, the IMF thinks these numbers are conservative; and the numbers given here are at least six years old. What portion of a country's wealth moves off shore depends on how hostile that country's laws are to oligarchs. So the Boston Consulting Group estimated in 2010 that Latin Americans move 50% of their wealth, compared to 30% of Europeans, and 10% of North Americans.[72] Carl Levin, a US Senator who keeps a website on "Closing Tax Loopholes," said this in 2010:

> A sophisticated offshore industry, composed of a cadre of international professionals including tax attorneys, accountants, bankers, brokers, corporate service providers, and trust administrators, aggressively promotes offshore jurisdictions to U.S. citizens as a means to avoid taxes and creditors in their home jurisdictions. These professionals, many of whom are located or do business in the United States, advise and assist U.S. citizens on opening offshore accounts, establishing sham trusts and shell corporations, hiding assets offshore, and making secret use of their offshore assets here at home.[73]

Secrecy laws

Secrecy laws present another systemic problem for a state (of obvious advantage to oligarchs). Many countries enact such laws to protect against the disclosure of information about bank accounts, and corporations. Often so called 'shell corporations' are established, which have no particular financial activity in themselves, but are used to house other corporations whose activities may be illegal or suspect, which want to stay out of view. In the U.S., many entities are 'incorporated' in the two states which have secrecy laws, i.e. Delaware and Nevada.[74]

Growing campaign finances

Increasing campaign expenditures and contributions are a recent trend which further advances the power of oligarchs to influence legislation in their favor. The United States Supreme Court decision in Citizens United v Federal Election Commission (2010) ruled that there can be no limit on corporate campaign expenditures (or contributions). The Court has also decided (in 2013) to hear the case arguing to raise limits for individual political contributions. Many people believe there is already too much influence on lawmakers and legislation by those who have access to the resources of the wealth defense industry, as we have said.

"Tax opinion letters"

These complex opinions are arguments presented by law firms to the Internal Revenue Service, to persuade IRS judges to rule in favor of their claims regarding tax obligations. As we all know, the IRS can reject a citizen's tax returns for one reason or another, and the tax payer can argue her case in turn. For ordinary citizens, the decisions are made according to clear published rules, and the outcomes are not too controversial, although they may ruffle feathers. But in the appeals made by agents of Ultra High Net Worth Individuals (i.e. oligarchs), the applicable rules are opaque and ambiguous, and allow for a great deal of interpretation. Furthermore, the IRS doesn't have enough funds, time or personnel, or in many cases even the legal sophistication to mount an effective argument, so the case is decided in favor of the oligarch. In complex cases a single "tax letter" can cost more than a million dollars. To illustrate the complexity of the issue, we could examine the record of such cases and appeals, which are reported in the annual "Standard Federal Tax Reporter" published by the Commerce Clearing House. In 1939, the record contained about 500 pages; in 2010 in contained over 70,000 pages (20 volumes)! Which poor, overworked IRS lawyer could hope to master the relevant data, principles and precedents to prosecute her case effectively?[75]

Uncertainty

The language of the tax code is written with a lot of room for interpretation, which is to the advantage of the oligarchs (and their agents in the wealth defense industry). The more holes there are in the relevant laws, the more room for litigation, and the better the chances of winning the appeal against the government. Many people argue in favor of simplifying the so-called tax code, but it is obvious that the lobbyists of the industry have a great deal to lose if that happens.[76] I'm reminded of a top-ten pop hit of Bobby Fuller in 1966: "I fought the law, and the law won." That is the usual outcome, for ordinary folks; anything else is only the stuff of romantic imagination (and oligarchy).

The "1%" versus the "1/100th of 1%"

It is useful to note that the phrase 'The 1%," which has gotten so much media attention since the start of the 2007 recession, is not at all one unified group. For instance, those who earn $400,000, and those who earn $400,000,000 pay the same marginal tax rate, although the latter's income is a thousand times as great as the former's. This is one proof of the effectiveness of the wealth defense industry.[77]

It may sound strange, but there are ways of quantifying the 'power' that wealth provides, in the sense of what resources can be mustered by the very wealthy, in order to influence laws and social environment that favor them. I'm not talking about bribes, or 'buying influence' directly, which no doubt happens, but about paying lobbyists, paying for "tax opinion letters", paying for litigation that forestalls implementing unfavorable legislation, and of course for relentless ad campaigns which convince the public to believe the myths and elect the legislators that support them.

To define 'oligarchs' in terms of the quantity of their wealth is vague. The main point is whether or not a person has the means to hire the services of the industry to defend that wealth. Industry agents think and speak in terms of how much investable financial assets clients have. Those with $2 million are called 'high net worth individuals' (HNWI), and those with $30 million are called 'ultrahigh net worth individuals' (UHNWI).

The following table shows the "material power index" of these 'super-wealthy' persons, as well as the 'merely wealthy' and other wealth categories we have been discussing. I use data from Winters, based on incomes in 2007, rounded for ease of comparison. The standard index number is 1, assigned to the average taxpayer in the bottom ninety percent.[78]

Material Power Index

Threshold of taxpayers	Number of taxpayers	Average income	Material Power-Index
Top 400	400	$345,000,000	10,000
Top 1/100th of 1%	14,500	$26,000,000	800
Top 1/10th of 1%	135,000	$4,000,000	125
Top 1%	750,000	$500,000	15
Top 10%	7,500,000	$128,000	4
Bottom 90%	135,000,000	$32,000	1

Political conservatives typically complain of "too much governmental regulation" of ordinary businesses, which is understandable. But they would do well to understand where better, if not more regulation is needed; it can serve their business and personal interests too, as well as those of the less advantaged, or those with less interest or skill in genuine entrepreneurial creativity. With that in mind, I'll characterize some of the popular myths which are promoted as part of the wealth defense industry's *modus operandi*.

Myths about America that favor the oligarchy

Every country has its myths. Many of them are just expressions of people's desire to think well of themselves, and to take a positive view of the future. At the same time, diversity in populations tends to pit groups against each other. And governments have always known the advantage of encouraging ideas that help them, and suppressing ideas that don't, by whatever means available, including censoring speech and killing dissenters and reporters of bad news.

The oligarchy adds another dimension to thought control, by means of its power to influence people without getting into the political fray directly. In America, oligarchs can steer public opinion by controlling media, launching ad campaigns, establishing schools, institutes and think tanks, and supporting spokes persons who frame the discussion and create the stories to work in their favor. I believe Americans are particularly susceptible to propaganda at all levels.[79]

Without wanting to create straw men to knock down, I'll characterize a few general ideas I often read and hear (in ads, talk shows, news, entertainment, 'blogs', coffee shop conversations, social media, etc.) which act as myths to help the oligarchic cause. Some of these are 'pro' (i.e. favor attitudes and conditions that would benefit oligarchy); others are 'con' (i.e. oppose attitudes and conditions that would restrict oligarchy).

America is the land of opportunity

This notion is a generic sales pitch that is especially pushed when people begin to get restless about bleak conditions that seem beyond their control. When particular problems are brought up, a stock answer is something like, "If it's so bad, why does the rest of the world want to immigrate here?" There's an appeal to this pseudo-argument; but then we learn why people do come here, or try to, and how unhappy are their conditions at home, which our middle classes would never tolerate. Perhaps the myth sayers might think that the disadvantaged foreigners should have stayed home and tolerate the bad conditions, or else tolerate them here and not try to change things for the better.

Anyone who works hard can make it

This myth of "upward mobility" is a common element of many other myths outlined here. The belief is very strong, which suggest it plays into some natural tendency to hope for the best, as I mentioned above. In fact it also supports the thesis that if you're having problems, don't blame the system, and certainly don't blame the oligarchs. If you're not successful, it's your fault. This myth is even accepted by those at the bottom who are very unlikely to succeed. It's a view that tends to keep people from making efforts at reforming the system. The common thought is, "I won't vote for limits or heavier burdens on the top tier since I could belong to that group at any time." The tenacity of this myth is nicely summarized in a *Wikipedia* article on "socioeconomic mobility".[80]

> Belief in strong social and economic mobility – that Americans can and do rise from humble origins to riches – has been called a "civil religion"[81], "the bedrock upon which the American story has been anchored",[82] and part of the American Dream, celebrated in the lives of famous Americans such as Benjamin Franklin and Henry Ford, and in popular culture (from the books of Horatio Alger and Norman Vincent Peale to the song "Movin' on Up"). Opinion polls show this belief to be both stronger now in America than in years past, and stronger than in other developed countries. However, in recent years several large studies have found that vertical inter-generational mobility is lower, not higher, in America than in those countries. The Brookings Institution said in 2013 that income inequality was increasing and becoming permanent, sharply reducing social mobility.[83]

The facts that sociologists have been reporting for decades show lower class citizens in America are increasingly unlikely to move into the middle class, let alone move high on the ladder. One hears of many 'success stories' that allegedly support the myth, yet we know that a few cases – even when well documented – don't show the general trends. I think it is largely this myth which keeps public opinion from supporting progressive tax rates. For example, when Congress first started debating the issue in 2010, polls favored extending "the Bush tax cuts" for everyone, regardless of income. And when the cuts were made permanent in 2012, the tax for the top income group (incomes over $400,000) moved up to 39.6% where it had been before the cuts. One could hardly call this progressive.[84]

Finally, we might mention a recent social phenomenon that seems widespread: people "fake" being well off. They buy stylish clothes, carry smart phones, and present themselves on Facebook pages in ways that emulate the popular notions of success. The entertainment industry keeps people distracted and deluded about their status and prospects in the society, by casino sounds and glittering TV studios, and by 'reality shows' about the lives and opinions of rich and famous movie actors, musicians, athletes and comics. It brings to mind the "bread and circuses" of ancient Roman.

A rising tide lifts all boats

This is a nice metaphor, but it's ambiguous. If it means every citizen benefits from an improving economy, that's not necessarily the case, as I'll show below. If it means we should support policies that facilitate the great enrichment of a few people, who will then distribute their largesse to those lower on the wealth ladder – that is at best naïve. If it refers to "supply side" economics, such as began in the Reagan administration, it's a policy that favors the wealthy. It's a theory that advancing the supply of goods (and the money to make them) rather than stimulating the demand, is best for the economy; and this is best accomplished by lowering taxes (income and especially capital gains), and easing governmental restrictions and regulation of banking and investment practices. This approach – disparagingly called 'trickle down' economics by its opponents, or as I might put it, the Biblical "crumbs that fall from the rich man's table" – has generally been discredited, especially after the global financial crisis (GFC), which started in mid-2007, and the ongoing international recession that followed.[85]

We have free market capitalism here

I've already pointed out that the neo-classical ideal of Adam Smith's viewpoint doesn't exist anywhere, and should not. But the point I'm emphasizing here is that those who speak in favor of free markets do whatever they can to distort the markets in their favor. They don't really want free markets. This is particularly true of executives who work, not for the success of their enterprises, but for their personal advantage, which they try to insure even to the detriment of their firms and the buying public. And this distortion is particularly true in the financial sector, where we have seen bail outs of banks that are 'too big to fail,' firms that have been left with unmanageable debt, and executive officers better off after the changes, despite their poor records.[86] We'll examine this more closely at the end of this chapter on oligarchy.

Rich people create jobs

It seems rather obvious that it takes money to employ people, and a lot of money to employ a lot of people. However, it is generally businesses rather than individuals which do the employing. The personal wealth of the business owner(s) is a separate issue from the capacity to employ, or the success at employment of the business they own. That being said, being rich doesn't cause a person or a business to employ others, nor does employing others always enrich the employer.

A rich employer can cut wages, or let employees go, or not employ them in the first place, as easily as hiring them. There is no fixed correlation between employment and wealth of business owners. The issue is whether the businesses which do employ are successful and continue to employ; and whether successful businesses always benefit the job market, by how many jobs they create, and what compensation employees are offered.

Having said this, I think it's true that the oligarchy of whom we've been speaking – i.e. the wealthiest persons – are typically not good for employment, in the economic sense. First, they are often not creators of jobs, contrary to what the myth implies, although they may move in the world of businesses which do employ people. For instance, they may be in private equity firms – something for which Mitt Romney was noted in the last U.S. presidential campaign. As such, they typically buy up, merge, reorganize, refinance and sell off businesses. As often as not, this process involves 'down-sizing' and other 'efficiency' measures including lay-offs. Secondly, very wealthy persons may, as I said earlier, be in the so-called FIRE sector (Finance, Insurance and Real Estate). They may be bankers, or invest in municipal bonds, or purchase land for development, none of which activities employs many people, relative to the large profits they generate for the owners.

Undocumented immigrants take from citizens

It's often said that illegal immigrants depress wages and use up social services intended for citizens. This idea seems to have support from all political sides, which is strange. Some politicians on the conservative side, such as Sen. John Cornyn of Texas, say they will not support 'immigration reform,' until the government has "full operational control" of the border, which would demand a great deal more money being devoted to that project.[87] In my view this plays into the American habit of xenophobia, and is a distraction. Since sealing up the border is a practical impossibility, it could excuse taking no further action to allow immigrants into the regular work force. If businesses such as fast food, landscape maintenance, cleaning services and farming actually benefit from laborers who are not protected by government labor laws, I assume they don't really want the flow to stop. On the other hand, the underclass of Americans may feel their tax supported assistance programs may be threatened by immigrants, yet the latter generally pay payroll taxes, as well as sales taxes, which go to those services.

Labor unions may believe that their wages are threatened as well. This is not true. The growth of the economy is not a zero-sum game. As more skills and more well employed workers come into the economy, the better are the conditions and opportunities for everyone. In my view, immigrants from Central and South America, as well as from Asia, South Asia, Africa, Eastern Europe and other places, bring energy and creative skills that are sorely needed. Aside from what cultural wealth they can bring, their legal admission into the country would provide general economic improvement to a society which is steadily losing its middleclass base in industries that require modern skills and knowledge. Immigrants can bring those skills which our educational system is not developing well. Presently, the biggest growth, in terms of employment and income possibilities, are in computer and digital technology, health care and biotechnology, energy and mining, followed by retail sales, management and services, automobile sales and marketing, construction specialties, and transportation.[88] These are open to all who gain the skills.

Governmental (social) programs sap the economy

Apart from the defense budget, which represents over half of so-called "discretionary spending," the main objects of scorn and negative publicity by conservatives are the non-military parts of the discretionary budget, together with so-called 'entitlements' which are mandatory, and cannot be cut in ordinary budget negotiations. Projected discretionary expenses for 2014 in round numbers are: Health and Human Services – $78 billion; Education – $71 billion; HUD – $33 billion; Justice – $16 billion; and "other" – $422 billion

– which includes things like State Department ($50 billion), Agriculture ($24 billion) and Interior ($12 billion). Mandatory expenditures include: Social Security ($860 billion), Medicare ($504 billion), Medicaid ($267 billion), and Debt interest ($223 billion). Total federal expenditures in 2014 are estimated to be $3.8 trillion, which is 23% of GDP. I recommend Christopher Chantrill's summary of U.S. federal budget categories, and expenditures made in recent years: "US Federal Budget FY13 Estimated Spending" for a convenient, interactive source of information.[89] Although I cannot find an independent assessment of Chantrill's objectivity, his figures are confirmed by other sources.[90] By his own report, he is a 'conservative,' and there may be some bias when he uses some categories – e.g "welfare" – in a way that is not duplicated by government terminology. In any case, these are the programs, plus the retirement benefits of 1.9 million retired military personnel in the defense budget, which receive the greatest negative press from the political right.

For reasons already summarized above, conservative critics often seem to disparage government in general, publicly. (By 'conservatives' in the context of spreading these myths, I mean primarily those trying to conserve, and expand, the wealth and power of the oligarchy, through advertising campaigns and favorable legislation – and those who buy into the myths). This general criticism of government is contagious; it plays into the feelings of many citizens who are frustrated by corruption, bureaucratic inefficiency, inadequate services, and their sense of being unable to advance, or in cases, even maintain what they had. Stories regularly circulate about great sums being given to 'welfare queens;' about food stamps being used for booze and candy, or sold on the street; about deserving white students' requests for financial aid, or admission to college, being passed over in favor of minority students; about Medicaid and Medicare fraud; about aid going to foreign populations instead of our own needy; about the absurdity of bi-lingual classes which serve immigrants – the list is endless. I'm sure many of these complaints have some basis in fact, but again, the anecdotal accounts - even when true - don't tell what is happening in the aggregate scale. This makes it hard to judge the value or disvalue to society, or the justice or injustice, or practical advisability of the public programs.

Our health care is the best without government in it

The U.S. does have world-class health care services. Unfortunately the system is very inefficient, and the result is its users pay more per capita – almost twice as much – as any other developed nation. Furthermore the resulting national state of health is mediocre by international standards. This is well summarized by a white paper from Thompson-Reuters, published in 2010[91] already cited. More importantly, the system has left many poor and young people totally without access. The recent national legislation called the Affordable Care Act (nick-named "Obama Care") has brought out the most virulent opposition from the political right, and continuing promises to repeal the whole thing. The efforts to have the act declared unconstitutional failed. Reasons for this opposition are, on the part of ordinary people, the belief that 'socialized medicine' will be inefficient, will ration medical care, will generate long waits, and will eliminate individual provider-patient relations – all part of the myth-making which has been in place since the New Deal era. I think that the reasons oligarchs encourage the myth are that any government control threatens insurance company's and providers' access to rising health care costs, and leaves potential employees less under pressure to accept jobs, whose medical benefits are at the discretion of employers. I'll have more to say about this topic in the section below on "fiscal policy and public purpose".

Teachers' unions are harming public schools

There is little disagreement from any sector that public school education in cities, which serves lower class students, has degenerated in recent decades. As many as half of high school students drop out, and those who graduate can't expect decent employment, let alone continuing to college. Students from wealthy public school districts, and from private schools, do reasonably well. At the university level, top tier institutions are well thought of internationally. In fact many of their students are from abroad; but most public school graduates are unprepared to meet their admission standards, not to mention the costs. At the public universities, costs are also increasing greatly, and students who have taken out school loans are defaulting in high numbers; some analysts say this may be leading to our next economic bubble. Student loan debt has tripled in the last decade to almost $1 trillion.[92]

In effect, there is a two-tier structure to schooling, and it's safe to say it will not 'level the playing field' in the society at large. Those who are in the lowest socio-economic class will most likely remain there. Education will not change this fact, because schools also reflect the divide between those who succeed and those who don't. I'll return to the topic of education in the next to last chapter of this essay.

Federal educational programs are inappropriate

Conservatives are quite generally opposed to the federal government oversight and funding of education, which they say should be the responsibility of state and local agencies. Some legislators advocate abolishing the office of Secretary of Education, which became a separate part of the President's cabinet only in 1979. President Reagan did not support the suggestions of his own Secretary, T. H. Bell, to appoint a Commission on Excellence in Education, so Bell did so himself. It published "A Nation at Risk" in 1983, which has been influential, and was followed up by another report – "A Nation Still At Risk" – in 1998, by then Secretary W. J. Bennett.

There are several reasons for this conservative opposition to federal education involvement, I think. They are political, although they may be expressed in principled terms. First, it will lessen the federal tax burden. Second, it will prevent across the board educational standards, and this in turn will allow individual states to compete with each other by training children in ways that can make them attractive to employers – primarily as purchasers of domestic goods, and as lower scale wage earners. Third, this will encourage private and privileged schools to develop higher skills for science, technology and management to fit the markets' needs at home and internationally. I am reminded of a statement that Jesse Jackson once made to the effect that 'It's cheaper to put a young man from the inner city into college for a year than to keep him in prison for a year.' The idea is clever and catchy, but the logic is bad. One for one, yes, a year of college is cheaper than a year of prison. But putting all the underclass kids in college would cost a great deal more than incarcerating the relatively small number of those who get into trouble with the law.

Colleges, especially the most prestigious, often advance the goals of oligarchs who are well aware of the fact. They may even contribute to the institutions and programs related to business. Sad to say, there is little support for music or the arts (except the commercial art and technology of film and advertising), or humanities, history or social sciences. So-called growth industries, which serve the interests of both oligarchs and those in lower classes, require higher levels of knowledge and training than in the past. Public and private universities can provide the education for these 'knowledge-based' industries. Critics of government involvement in education typically fail to acknowledge the federal subsidies which already go to colleges and universities – especially to the most prestigious private universities associated with the high growth markets.

Public policies provide direct grants, tax breaks, military contracts, patent rights and other support to organizations, educators, inventors and venture capitalists who come together in communities to develop their ideas and products. Silicon Valley is the name known world-wide, which includes San Jose, San Francisco and Oakland

California, and connects to Stanford University and Berkeley. It is still the leader, but there are many others, e.g. in Seattle (with the University of Washington), in Cambridge (with Harvard and Yale), in Washington DC (with George Washington University), and in Dallas, San Diego, Philadelphia, Atlanta, Chicago, Durham NC and thirty or forty more cities around North America – each associated with one or more major universities. Some of these specialize in particular industries (like digital and internet technology, medical and biotechnology, or mining and energy), and the professions associated with them (engineering, medicine, business and law).[93]

Unions are bad for the economy

This myth extends the dislike of unions in public sector jobs (e.g. teachers and firefighters) to the private sector. The claim depends on both of the meaning of 'good', and of 'economy.' If measured only in terms of wages, it seems obvious that they are typically increased by union negotiations. Does this lower the competitiveness of US firms? Apparently it does for certain industries, such as cars, steel, and more recently electronics, which either lost market share to foreign producers, or moved abroad to take advantage of cheaper labor industry. But higher wages benefit wage earners, and encourage affected industries to be more efficient, or find new products which meet the higher wage market. It has always been a conflict of interests. It's interesting that Canada (with 28%), Germany (with 18%) and Finland (with 70%) have much higher levels of unionization than the U.S., yet seem to be doing well at home and overseas.[94]

If 'good for the economy' is measured simply in terms of GDP, the economy has grown in recent decades without the help of unions. But as said, it has been limited for the most part to the FIRE sector which doesn't help lower tier employees. There are presently some eleven million unemployed US workers, and those who are employed have wages that have generally remained stagnant. But the direct effect of unions and of right-to-work laws on employment is very difficult to analyze, and the results seem inconclusive. The 'myth' we are discussing here seems clearly to have been accepted by the general public, since both union membership and employment have suffered; the sources and goals of the campaign to propagate the myth are easy to find.

'Right to work' laws exist in twenty-four states – most in the southeast, south and southwest – typically farm states, or those with large populations of poor, underemployed or migrant workers. In 2012 Michigan and Indiana joined this group. The phrase 'right to work' is a euphemism for laws that limit unions' influence by prohibiting them from contracting with employers to make membership and paying dues conditions of employment. This weakens their ability to bargain effectively, which is of course their purpose. Political organizations like the National Right to Work Committee and the National No Rights At Work Legal Attack Foundation are supported by conservative billionaires like the Koch, Coors and DeVos families.[95]

In any case, it is clear that the public has bought the myth, and opinion has turned against unions generally in recent decades. Union enrollment has declined steadily, from a high of 50% in the 1950's to just over 11% last year, which was the figure back in 1917. The percent of unionized public-sector workers, which includes police, firemen and teachers, is almost six times that of private sector workers. At the time of the recent public disputes about right-to-work in Michigan and Indiana, public support was running 74% in favor of such laws. And immediately after the passage of those laws, union membership in these two states fell even further.[96]

It seems safe to say that the reason for this decline in union membership is the undoing of government regulations which protect employees from being exploited by those who benefit from the lowest labor costs. Generally this means one can expect to see media campaigns opposing any efforts to regulate the social effects of so called 'free market forces,' for example by laws regarding minimum wages, maximum hours, compensation for injury, retirement plans, health care, unemployment insurance, safety regulations, and so forth – all part of the image of the bad Big Brother government. It is not surprising that public employee unions (e.g. teachers) are being attacked too, with particular vehemence, since not only their 'benefits,' but their entire wage structure depends on taxes which burden business firms even more.[97]

National debt kills economic growth

I will discuss this idea below, in the chapter on Modern Money under 'National debt and inflation', and showed why the myth is false. A very recent blog by J. D. Alt explains clearly the principles and usefulness of 'fiat money' and the error of the concern about national debt, which is driving 'austerity' programs in all branches of government.[98] Here I'll only mention an interesting controversy over the effects of national debt on economic growth.

In 2010, two Harvard economists, Carmen Reinhart and Kenneth Rogoff, published a study that showed a connection between high public debt and diminished GDP growth which influenced, or at least was cited in, political policy statements supporting austerity (e.g. in the Republican Party's "Ryan Budget" proposal in the United States, and by soon-to-be Chancellor of the Exchequer George Osborne in the UK.)[99] But in 2013, several economists from the University of Massachusetts at Amherst - Thomas Herdon, Michael Ash, and Robert Pollin - published findings that contradicted Reinhart and Rogoff, and pointed out errors in data gathering.[100] It now seems that the 'common sense' presumption of the negative effects of debt (as Sen. Paul Ryan put it) are not proven by experience. But more importantly, the controversy has shown the public that the direction of 'causality' between the two variables is not known. Does debt cause lower growth, or does lower growth cause debt, or does it go both ways?

The 'military-industrial-complex' helps the economy

Paradoxically, while government is being critiqued and vilified in public (by media spokespersons, advertising campaigns, and various think tanks and foundations), behind the scenes, as we have already pointed out, legislators are wooed by wealth-defending lobbyists, tax lawyers, *et al*, trying to win them over to their viewpoint. And certainly not all government spending is inimical to oligarchic interests. Military spending is a government program generally encouraged by conservatives.

More than sixty years ago, in his farewell address of 1961, President Eisenhower warned his fellow citizens, "We must guard against the acquisition of unwarranted influence, whether sought or unsought, by the military-industrial complex." Some call it the military-industrial-congressional complex, since it involves mutually overlapping areas of benefit to leaders in military, business and political circles. There is a never-ending opportunity to take advantage of this collusion. It is a striking fact of history that the United States has been engaged in military conflicts, greater or lesser, for all its history; the nation was begotten in a war. For more than half its history, US conflicts were generally with European powers (England, France and Spain), either against colonial intrusion, or to expand into the territories owned by colonial powers in the 'new world,' like Louisiana, California and Mexican-owned Texas. America also had to fight internal, localized conflicts among its own people, as well as the great Civil War. But in the last hundred years, U.S. "actions" have been "extraterritorial"; in many cases they have involved interests half way around the world.

I won't try to judge whether the United States is a belligerent nation, although I believe so, as do many others, non-Americans and Americans alike. Ordinary citizens here typically support whatever action the government initiates in these matters. Every government tries to justify its military actions, to its own people at least. In any case, in the past century our "military operations" great and small have gone on without any pause – sometimes in several places simultaneously. The list of these actions is striking to read, and bound to make one pause. The *Wikipedia* "Timeline of US military operations" briefly discusses 316 of them throughout our 240-year history, which averages to more than 13 every decade. These operations included 12 protracted wars – one every 20 years on average.[101] Although we're asking whether military spending is good for the economy, we can't lose sight of the larger question of the value of war, against which the monetary issues must be judged. Christopher Hedges, an editor and wartime correspondent for NYT commented on this in 2010 while the U.S. was engaged in two war zones.

> If we really saw war, what war does to young minds and bodies, it would be impossible to embrace the myth of war. If we had to stand over the mangled corpses of schoolchildren killed in Afghanistan and listen to the wails of their parents, we would not be able to repeat clichés we use to justify war. This is why war is carefully sanitized. This is why we are given war's perverse and dark thrill but are spared from seeing war's consequences. The mythic visions of war keep it heroic and entertaining...[102]

I can't imagine making a serious effort at 'cost-benefit analysis' of a war proposal – at least not publicly – although one can estimate the strictly financial costs, by looking at defense department expenses, and by comparing Private Sector and Public Sector balances in war years. The numbers are difficult to analyze, however, because it requires defining what is meant by 'defense related'. By some estimates, the total defense expenditures should include military pensions, intelligence gathering by NSA, and other indirect costs. There is also a variable element called "overseas contingency" that accounts for ongoing operations (e.g. the current war in Afghanistan which is winding down). It also can include Veterans Affairs,

Homeland Security, and spending in other agencies that support defense, which the Defense Department does not count directly. One estimate puts total costs in 2012 as between $1 trillion and $1.4 trillion.[103]

For FY 2014, trimmed down military expenses are expected to be about $780 billion, using numbers from the Office of Management and Budget (OMB), although some of the recent proposed cutbacks may well be overturned by Congress members whose constituents count on military spending in their areas.[104] This amount represents 20% of the total federal budget, and about 5% of GDP. It is more than the total combined defense budgets of the next seventeen countries.[105]

But is the military-industrial complex 'good for the economy'? That depends, of course, on one's evaluation of its activities. It employs over 1.5 million active service personnel, over 1 million national guard members, and 750,000 civilian workers (in its "base budget"), which makes it the world's largest employer.[106]The relevant question is whether they are employed efficiently and to the benefit of the society, and whether non-military expenditures could do as well or better. Depending on how quickly she or he advances in rank, a basic enlisted person, with no special skills to start with, can expect to be paid perhaps $30,000 yearly, and $75,000 after ten years; and of course her food, clothing, shelter and all medical care are provided. She can expect additional "allowances" for housing, if married, and for overseas deployment and hazardous duty. With special skills, the rates increase. Short term servers receive educational benefits, and career people have generous retirement benefits.[107]

From the perspective of employment, then, the military establishment seems like a good investment of federal funds, while it maintains the necessary national defense. However, we should keep this budget in perspective. Expenditures for military personnel are about $150 billion, out of the total defense budget of $780 billion. The rest of the money goes to R&D, procurement, construction, "operations and maintenance" and activities of civilian contractors, all of which are notoriously inefficient and subject to fraud. The benefit goes to firms and individuals at the top of the wealth scale. Again, it is a matter of whose interests the myth serves.

GDP proves we are doing well

In the political disputes over fiscal policies each side likes to look for evidence that their side is right. News media typically report economic growth by citing GDP numbers. Such reports imply that the national economy is doing well when GDP is rising. But this assumption is often false, for at least two reasons. First, these numbers represent aggregate financial wealth, even when they are given in terms of 'per capita' income. They say nothing about how the assets are distributed in the society – to real, not 'average,' citizens. It is not only possible, but true, that ordinary citizens are no better off, or in some groups are less well off, than they were several decades ago. In fact, average wage incomes have remained the same, and people at the bottom are worse off (if we discount public sector programs to help the disadvantaged). During the same time, the wealth of top citizens has increased greatly. For example, in the last thirty years (1979 to 2007), earnings of the top one percent grew 156 percent, and those of top $1/10^{th}$ of one percent grew 362 percent; while earnings of the lowest 90 percent of earners grew 17 percent.[108]

The second reason why GDP is not a good measure of societal prosperity is more subjective. GDP doesn't take into effect the 'value' of non-measurable goods, like the safety and attractiveness of the environment, the friendliness of the neighbors, or the quality of education and health services of different regional and demographic areas.

Predatory capitalism and money-value

"In the name of God and profit" is one of the quotes I put as epigraphs to this essay. It was said by a 14th century Italian textile merchant named Francesco Datini; he inscribed it on all his ledgers. By

comparison, 20th century economist Milton Friedman said that the "social responsibility of business is to increase its profits".[109] Both of these men knew that money was not the highest value. Datini put God above it. And Friedman knew, and argued, that capitalism is for the service of society. His idealistic point was that businesses best serves the society when it gives people what they want, at the best prices, without imposing the owners' values on the public. In effect, people vote with their purchases, and if they don't like what some businesses do (such as pollute, or endanger employees' health), they can pass laws to that effect. This, I believe, is what he *meant*, but unfortunately he said that 'increasing profits' was the goal. Indeed, today profit (i.e. money) does seem to be the goal, which is very worrying to me.

By contrast to these two men – two supporters of capitalism – money has apparently become the dominant cultural value, under the influence of what is sometimes called "predatory capitalism." I believe this is one of the effects of oligarchy in recent decades, about which I'll offer a few summary comments. The first is that it's nothing new or surprising that people pay attention to making enough money for their everyday needs; very few Americans could live off the land today. And I doubt that even 'survivalists' would prefer that life.

People at the bottom of the income scale might be expected to think more about money than those better off, since their existence is more hand to mouth. Casual observation suggests that they may actually think about it less than more affluent. A sense of frustration can lead people to try to put money out of their minds, at least temporarily. Instead of making plans and developing the means to pay for the necessities and the extras they desire, they may try to ignore debts (phone and utility bills, student loans, rental payments, medical bills, IOUs to siblings and friends), and wait to meet each service cutoff or dunning call as it comes along. Paradoxically, they may spend their limited cash on a concert, or going out with friends to a bar. Although this approach is irrational and saddens me, I sympathize, and think I understand. It's perhaps what psychologists like to call 'denial'.

At the middle-income level, money seems to have crowded out other traditional non-monetary values to an increasing degree. Since the 1990's, a growing proportion of college students give as their primary reasons for higher education getting a good job and making money. For those oriented this way, some also realize the importance not just of college training, but of attending a prestigious school. Apparently the curriculum really doesn't matter. As one student commented, in recent polls at UCLA, "At those schools, it doesn't really matter what you studied or how well you did. Goldman Sachs will hire Art History majors out of Yale all day long." Another said,

> I wonder if this has any connection at all to the fact that [the] President, in his Inaugural Address, declared the whole point of college is "training workers", and that we should do more to make sure that immigrants who want to be "engineers" should get to stay and go to college.
>
> Critical thinking? Intellectual inquiry? Literature, art, music? Nope. "Training workers."[110]

Christopher Hedges, in *The Death of the Liberal Class*, makes strong arguments to show that the traditional institutions which until recently have encouraged people to think about non-monetary values, have themselves been co-opted by money interests. Government, academia, the arts, the press, and even churches, show the dominance of money values. One can even say they have all been 'bought out.'[111]

Relatedly, the quest for money seems to encourage corruption at all levels. I'm often amazed to see persons of great wealth take great risks of exposure, and some fall to ruin because of their uncontrolled desire for wealth. Bernie Madoff is one high profile example. But there are many who evade the law, although their behavior seems clearly contrary to their official obligations. Recent bank frauds illustrate this. Charles H. Smith wrote about this in a blog last year. First, he pointed out, as I suggested above, "There are two key social control myths in America: one, that everyone is equal before the law, and two, that similar fundamental opportunities are available to all."[112] Smith suggests we should replace these myths with the following "hypotheses" which he believes to be true:

> When the system enables fraud, collusion, misrepresentation of risk, moral hazard (the separation of risk and gain) and embezzlement, then it also rewards them.
>
> When the rule of law is routinely bypassed, flouted, negated or simply ignored without triggering uniformly applied consequences, then the system is thoroughly, totally, completely, hopelessly corrupt.

Smith gives examples to show that the two 'social control myths' are false, in the realm of oligarchic interactions with government. There are many stories and discussions of what might be called 'legal corruption' but my impression is they don't often get into the mainstream media, or catch public interest. Matt Taibbi's article in *Rolling Stone*, "Secrets and Lies of the Bank Bailout," is one exception that got well-earned attention.[113]

Chapter Six

Debt, Wealth and Democracy

Democracy - the group v. the individual

Although we haven't focused on the fact so far, all the issues we have considered involve an unstated, and perhaps unrecognized conflict that exists in every group, from family to nation. It is simply this. People are born self-interested. As Hobbes pointed out famously, life in the 'state of nature' is "solitary, poor, nasty, brutish and short". Of course, there are no people who have ever lived in such a natural state, despite their natural tendencies. Everyone lives in some society or other, no matter how 'primitive'. Even so, the question has always been how to make an orderly society out of naturally disorderly individuals.

As I noted above, Rene Girard believes religion is the first way of bringing order to every primal group, even though religious societies often perpetuate violence. Typically, small tribal groups have always been organized and controlled by elders who are experts in religious myths and rituals and the community follows their guidance. As groups become larger and more specialized, power is typically divided among religious leaders and non-religious leaders like chiefs with skill in war. And in still larger civilizations, the power has involved kings and prelates, or emperors and priestly supporters. Ordinary people were, and continue to be controlled through fear, either of the gods, or of earthly rulers, or both. This has been the case through all history until a radical new way of thinking about social order developed, when Greek and Roman thought were rediscovered in the 15th and 16th centuries, and rational empirical science developed in the 17th and 18th centuries.

Democracy is the name we give to this new approach to social order, but it is well to remember that democracy is not, nor has it ever been, a single clear concept; it has changed over time, and developed differently in Classical Greece and Republican Rome, in England, America, France, and other parts of the "Western World", and it continues today to grow in various forms in other struggling parts of the world, haltingly, and against strong opposition.

I bring up these commonplace facts of history to give a context for drawing some conclusions in this overview of money, debt and public purpose in America. The ideas summarized in Chapter 4 above suggest traditional and interpretive religious and moral principles by which a society and its members might well be guided. The ideas in Chapter 5 about oligarchic influence on the economy outlined a state of affairs that few could call fair or beneficial to the society. But we still have to examine what political structure would best assure that these principles may be put into practice. Many people in the world, and even whole nations, still support the idea of a 'religious' polity, and a government of religious laws. By contrast, our society has decided on a secular political structure, and democratic legal processes. The topic of this chapter is to analyze briefly, and raise some questions about that structure and those processes.

Why should there be a "new nation" at all?

The United States evolved from a collection of independent states which themselves were originally collections of various immigrant communities, of primarily Northern European protestant origin (e.g. English, Dutch, and German). All these colonial offspring were strongly anti-Catholic. The succession laws of England would not admit a Catholic monarch until 2013! What were the motives for founding the Virginia Company (by Walter Raleigh, under the Virgin Queen Elizabeth) in 1588, later to become the Plymouth Company and the London Company? Motives (at least in official statements) were first, to convert the native peoples to Protestant Christianity; second, to relieve great population pressures in England; and third, to provide sources of raw materials that were free of the problems of importing them from lands controlled by other countries.[114] And the settlements of "New England" competed with those of "New France" and "New Spain" for control of North America. Remember also that these beginnings were not only by the leave of the British monarchy, but also with its encouragement and support. Add to this, the monarchy itself was going through revolutionary changes, and royalty was in process of gradually ceding its control of government to parliamentary political forces.

To complicate matters further, the settlements of New England in the northeast were very different culturally from those that started in Jamestown (also English), where the emphasis was primarily agricultural, and slaves became a dominant issue, politically, economically and morally. To bring all these elements together, and construct a new nation was problematic from the beginning; and it certainly didn't have the full support of all the persons affected, either in Europe or the colonies. That's why one author has called the American 'revolutionary war' a 'civil war', involving Tories v Whigs, "both within the American Colonies and between the American Colonies and the United Kingdom."[115]

The United States is not a "religious nation"

Americans today show much more 'religiosity' than Europeans, according to many polls. Three quarters of Americans identify themselves as Christians – primarily Protestants. More than 50% claim that religion is 'very important' to them. Although this number has declined with time, it is still more than twice the rate of most European nations (except Poland, which is still largely Catholic). About a quarter of Americans are Catholic. Despite their negative views of gay rights contraception and abortion, most Catholics call themselves Democrats. By contrast, Evangelicals and fundamentalists, who are more concentrated in the West and South, tend to identify with conservative politics and the Republican Party. Midwest and Northeast Christians affiliate with the more liberal religions, or are without any affiliation, and identify with liberal politics and the Democratic party.[116]

Whatever are the reasons for this diversity and geographical distribution of beliefs, religious thinking has always played a big part in political campaigns, and in national government policy debates. For this reason it is a topic we should take into account, when trying to analyze the public good and the political mechanisms best suited to bring it about. As I never tire of saying, emotion gets in the way of good analysis; and I doubt if any topic generates more emotion than religion.

Religious conservatives in the U.S. like to say that ours is a religious – even a Christian – nation. They often express anger over what they see as a liberal bias against religion, when there are complaints registered about prayer in schools, or Christmas crèche scenes in town halls, or adding "One nation under God" to the Pledge of Allegiance in 1954.[117] Since our focus here is on public good and public policy, it's well to underscore the difference between public and private religious beliefs and practices. The First Amendment, which was ratified in 1791 as part of the Bill of Rights, states

"Congress shall make no law respecting an establishment of religion, or prohibiting the free exercise thereof." Over time, and against a lot of opposition, this Amendment's original limitation of Congress was extended, in a series of Supreme Court decision, to apply to state and local governments as well.

The "wall of separation between church and state", as it is often called,[118] is not a national rejection of religion in people's lives and opinions, but a prohibition of any governmental laws (or practices) that favor or disfavor any particular religious view, or religion in general. This practical policy was the result of long and thoughtful debate among the so-called Founders, especially Franklin, Adams, Washington, Jefferson and Madison. Steven Waldman's *Founding Faith* (2012) is a well-balanced and well-researched historical analysis of this topic, by a person sympathetic to religious beliefs.[119]

These five men came from widely different religious backgrounds, and due to their various experiences of religious abuse and bigotry, each changed his thinking over time. Franklin, the oldest of the group, left Puritan Boston for Quaker Pennsylvania (and Philadelphia), to be freer to publish a variety of viewpoints that he saw being argued – especially the new Deist perspective which he found attractive, and with which he generally agreed; but he had his own interpretation of it, as he did of most things. Franklin despised the Calvinist notion of faith only, and instead emphasized morality, virtue and action. "Imitate Jesus and Socrates," he suggested. Being realistic, he helped to change Pennsylvania's pacifist laws, so the state might support the revolution against England.

George Washington – a Virginian – watched his state (Anglican by law) persecute, or exclude Puritans, Catholics, Quakers, Indians and Jews. Perhaps a Universalist in his views – certainly a Mason – Washington was a non-sectarian. He believed that God intervenes in human affairs. He was cordial, but non-committal with regard to particular sects, and worked pragmatically to use religious beliefs in the support of his war efforts. Washington didn't seem interested in theological distinctions or philosophical arguments that engaged some of his fellow Founders. He knew religion was important to individual life, and the preservation of the society.

By contrast with Washington, Thomas Jefferson was a deep and critical humanist thinker, but he was not an atheist disbeliever. He expressed antagonism to organized religion, however, especially in relation to priestly control. He was notorious for having written his own version of the *Bible*, which excised any reference to supernatural events. He admired Jesus greatly for his principles of love and morality.

Jefferson's statement that 'he didn't care whether someone believed in one god or twenty' certainly didn't help his standing among the mainstream religions. Even so, his efforts to separate church and state helped the cause of minority groups, like the Baptists and other 'evangelicals', for which they honored him. In any case he had great confidence in reason, and believed that thoughtful humans could come to know God by seeing the inner workings of nature. As Waldman notes wryly, Jefferson's liberal fans might be surprised to know that he believed there is an "intelligent design".

John Adams, growing up and staying in Puritan New England, rejected the Puritan's bigotry, yet he never left the church. He studied religions at Harvard, and felt that a democracy – in the absence of monarchic rule – would need the influence of religion to keep order among citizens who are naturally self-interested and depraved. Despite what Waldman calls his inconsistencies, Adams remained with his church, but was a "militant Unitarian".

Madison was from an upper-class family in Virginia, and involved in church politics. He nevertheless had a very liberal education at a young age. For whatever reason, he bypassed the more usual and acceptable education offered at William and Mary College, and went to school in New Jersey, at what would later be called Princeton. His teachers and experiences there were influenced by the developing New Awakening, or evangelical movement, and by a general respect for sciences and classical humanities. Madison became what Waldman calls a "radical pluralist". He was the chief designer of the US Constitution, and the one who, as Virginia's representative to the new national government, introduced and argued for various amendments, now called the Bill of Rights, and saw them through committee discussions into acceptance by Congress, and final state ratification in 1791.

The First Amendment, then, was the result of a considered and pragmatic compromise among all the parties who were involved. What they shared was a belief that state support of any religion always tends towards abuse of outsiders, and that those religions which can't survive without governmental support are probably not vital.

Maximize individual freedom of choice and behavior

There is nothing to keep people from bringing their own religious views into political debates, to inform any discussion about any topic. But all viewpoints, including the non-religious, must be admitted into the argument. Furthermore, regardless of the thinking of the majority of those considering a proposal, there are limits to what they can impose on, or demand of the minority. That is to say, within reasonable limits, individual citizens must be given maximum freedom of viewpoint and way of life, so far as it doesn't harm others, even if their perspective is hated and opposed by all the rest in their community.[120] This certainly applies to religious belief and life. Where else it applies – i.e. what else may be a "civil right" – is a matter for continuing social, political and legal consideration and conflict, as we see every day.

Here is a simple example. Should a citizen have to wear a helmet when riding a motorcycle? Some states say yes, and some say no. But the principle is to maximize individual freedom. The only excuse for limiting the driver's choice would be that not wearing a helmet is a danger to others, or a threat to public welfare. It's conceivable that a serious head injury could lead to a public cost in terms of health care, or higher insurance rates. That might 'justify' such a law. Even so, under federal pressure, all but three states have enacted universal helmet wearing for motorcycles. On the other hand, adult bicyclists don't have to wear helmets in any state, although in some states, children must wear them.

Federalists and antifederalists

The search for a proper balance of the tensions between and among individuals, or between and among groups, or between individuals and groups, is an endless task. Framing the American Constitution was an effort to give a general structure in which these tensions may be resolved in a productive and orderly way. And the framers themselves had great disagreements. The only thing that was not in question, after seceding from Great Britain, was whether to adopt democracy. But a major tension remained over what democracy entailed. From the start, there were "federalists" at odds with "antifederalists", and some who worked for a compromise. The same tensions exist today, under different banners. Anyone interested in a rational solution to this debate would do well to read some of the early exchanges, particularly among Hamilton, Madison and Jefferson, both as collaborators, and as opponents.[121] *The Federalist* was a series of eighty-five essays supporting the proposed Constitution, published serially in New York papers in 1787 and 1788. To give a sense of their scope, here is a quote from Federalist No 1, by Hamilton who wrote the majority of the essays.

It has been frequently remarked, that it seems to have been reserved to the people of this country, by their conduct and example, to decide the important question, whether societies of men are really capable or not, of establishing good government from reflection and choice, or whether they are forever destined to depend, for their political constitutions, on accident and force.[122]

As I write this, the US Senate is once again arguing over changing 'filibuster rules' – i.e. whether it should take a simple majority or a two thirds majority – to end debate on any issue. This is a procedural matter. It has nothing to do about any particular debate over a substantive issue, but it has great influence on the outcomes of those debates.

Formation and problems of political parties

Conflict among individual citizens, or between individuals and the small groups to which they relate (family, neighbors, community, workmates, employers, teachers, those affected by zoning issues, etc.) are often matters for private negotiation or appeal to local authorities. More general issues and larger interest groups (farm workers, disabled persons, civil rights, border disputes, trade regulation, infrastructure, regional and national security, and so forth) push issues up to the state and federal level, for litigation or new legislation. But how these issues should be handled, and what level of government should handle which matters, have divided people into 'parties' – or interest groups – that reflect their ideals, and their personal, social and political aims. Today we have the Tea Party, Occupy Wall Street, The Rainbow Coalition, Green Peace, the National Rifle Association, Skin Heads, and so on. Some are formal and/ or legal; some are not.

For whatever reasons, in America these diverse interest groups have coalesced at the national level into just two major political parties. Although their names have changed over time, their 'character' is believed to have remained quite constant. This belief that a certain set of 'core values' defines the political parties can be problematic. Jefferson commented about parties ("sects" as he called them) in a letter in 1798, when he was Vice President under John Adams, two years before he became President himself.

> Two political Sects have arisen within the U. S. the one believing that the executive is the branch of our   government which the most needs support; the other that like the analogous branch in the English Government, it is already too strong for the republican parts of the Constitution; and therefore in equivocal cases they incline to the legislative powers: the former of these are called federalists, sometimes aristocrats or monocrats, and sometimes tories, after the corresponding sect in the English Government of exactly the same definition: the latter are styled republicans, whigs, jacobins, anarchists, disorganizers, etc. These terms are in familiar use with most persons.[123]

From Jefferson's remarks, we can see several historical facts that are relevant to US politics today. First, political parties are not part of the formal, constitutional structure of government; they arose as people saw the need. Second, they mirror in this country the political structure of English government, but with an important difference. Great Britain had (and has) a parliamentary structure, which allows for coalitions which reflect the diversity of interest groups there. Thirdly, the major difference between these parties, in Jefferson's judgment, was the division of power between the executive and legislative branches. This is still a hotly debated issue.

The origin of the conflict in England was the struggle for power between the king and his noble vassals in medieval times, which led first to the limiting of the king's power (in the Magna Carta, 800 years ago), and finally to the subordination of the king to 'the people' (following the 'glorious revolution' of 1688, and the Bill of Rights of 1689,[124] and the development of a constitutional monarchy over time). This path to democracy was long and halting, and the Founders were well aware of it. For Jefferson, the deeper issue of national parties was the conflict between the 'power of the people'(which is located in the Senate and House, which he calls "the republican parts") and the authority of the President to get things done thoughtfully and efficiently, without the constant interference of changing public opinion. As mentioned above, Hamilton and Madison had argued for the 'federalist' view, when they were trying to get a strong central government, to replace the original structure under the "Articles of Confederation". That debate itself must have been informed by the same skepticism of central government, which brought back memories of royal control.

In his letter, Jefferson is being sarcastic when he refers to advocates of more power to Congress (the 'republican' parts) as "jacobins, anarchists, disorganizers, etc." Jefferson himself was an advocate of the 'purer' notion of democracy, because he believed that ordinary people *can* chose well for themselves. Hamilton thought Jefferson was deluded in this belief, and under the sway of the radical French philosophers. Madison ended up siding with Jefferson, against Hamilton, but his view was a compromise. He thought people had to be guided by reason, and that they could learn from education and experience, how to take responsibility in governmental matters. It would be a tricky and difficult training program. These 'enlightenment' men were well aware of how emotional, violent and erratic 'the masses' can be, and easily led by demagogues (as they knew from history, and were observing in France).

"Constructing the political spectacle"

Jefferson's ideas in this letter bring to mind another point that is relevant to the present condition of American government, which I would call degenerating. It also speaks directly to our present discussion of an effective structure for maximizing both the public good, and individual rights. The two-party system can't possibly give realistic political expression to the diversity of conflicting interests in our society. But it can, and does provide an effective diversion for ordinary people, and a *symbolic structure* onto which they can project their personal beliefs and desires. It's very like the allegiance that fans have for 'their' team in baseball or football (or in Europe, soccer), and the outcomes of the contest have equally little effect on the practical issues of law making or everyday life. Political scientist Murray Edelman showed these ideas clearly fifty years ago in his study *The Symbolic Uses of Politics*, and confirmed them twenty five years later with a follow up study, *Constructing the Political Spectacle*.[125]

According to Murray, politicians express their goals and values in the most abstract and general possible language, without giving any details. In this way, their hearers can read them to mean anything they want. Symbolic or ritual activities are used to evoke visions or 'associations' which cannot be checked against reality. Voting and elections are good examples. The language of party platforms is used to gain membership; it doesn't affect behavior after elections. Campaign speeches are geared to the hopes and fears of particular audiences; they don't predict the behavior of the candidates. They seldom can be 'checked out' later for being true or false. In national political conventions, the whoop and holler, the balloons and confetti, the banners and flags, the *tete-a-tete* caucuses behind closed doors, the 'candid' remarks to reporters on the floor, the national anthem, the pledge of allegiance, the keynote speeches – are all parts of a long developed tradition. It is an almost religious dramatic ritual that gives a sense of grandeur, importance and inevitability to the election process, and allows the public to feel involved, even though its involvement is widely disconnected from the realities of government.

And on election day, after the voting (another symbolic ritual) with much speculation and commentary, and bated breath, and anxious watching of TV screens, the results are in. One combatant graciously accepts victory, the other graciously concedes defeat, and both parties confirm that 'the people have spoken'. Thus united by a higher public purpose, the parties return to the business of government – the business of carrying out the will of the people, dutifully and unavoidably. The last point is worth emphasis.

The 'business of government' is largely conducted by bureaucrats; most people realize this. They think this army of government agents and employees is a machine that is structured and impelled to carry out the decisions of lawmakers, who themselves 'represent' the popular will. This is another myth, as Edelman shows clearly. Governmental bureaucracies are not only inefficient; that is to be expected. Bureaucrats are individuals, and like other people in other jobs, they have their own agendas. Each of these can interpose particular private interests, pro or con, on the policies for which his or her agency is charged. There is as much variety here as there is in the nongovernmental population, who believe their will is being done in the policies of their favorite parties in or out of power.

I hope my ideas here are not taken as cynical. This is not all a grand conspiracy (although there is plenty of opportunistic mythmaking.) It's the nature of people in every society to see their government through filters of their own wishes and experience. Of course some people have always known how to take advantage of these facts of human nature. It is simply that people who wish to have a real effect on government, whether for good or ill, need to know how it is, and not how they wish to believe it is. They must work hard not to be 'remote,' even while feeling 'involved'. That's the role of awareness, information, and careful thought – not propaganda and self-delusion.

Political movements, party endorsements, choosing spokespersons, campaigns, conventions and precinct voting procedure, are all remote from the people – even from most of the citizens who volunteer to participate directly in the campaigns and go out actively to support their cause. This is particularly true as media dominate people's attention. Most Americans are political spectators, whose ideas and actions have little effect on the decisions and events that make real differences in their lives. Murray calls this separation of the state from the public "remoteness", which I think has only grown in the last three or four decades; paradoxically, this is the time of an explosion of "communication" technology, in mass media and now the internet.

When critics complain that the US government is dysfunctional, they have in mind that partisan politics, rather than congressional responsibility, is the primary motive in governmental interactions, and therefore the work of governing is left undone. The unending media chatter from "inside the Beltway" – i.e. Washington – is full of angry rhetoric, and accusations passed back and forth in "sound bites" (short phrases) that give no hint of reasoning, subtlety or possibility of compromise. That's because the politicians speak through the media, and appeal to the emotions of their constituents, to maintain their popularity and continuity in office. I've heard older congress members who have retired from office express regret that there is little civility or personal contact among the politicians in recent times, because they have little chance to socialize informally. They don't typically live with families in the Capitol, but work a short week and fly home to families and friends for long weekends and meetings with constituents. And their constituencies are in districts that are 'gerrymandered' into being totally of one party or interest group. This leads to extremism and inflexibility among the representatives.

I don't know the motives of politicians (or anyone else). Perhaps they are concerned for the public good. And perhaps they do genuinely collaborate with their colleagues, out of sight of the public, to bring about laws they think are just. But the system in which they operate is damaged by the pervasive and corrupting influence of money values; and the general public, which should be the ultimate arbiter of governmental policies in a democratic republic, is largely ignorant. It can't do its job of self-governing, even if it wanted to.

Is the federal government too big?

No one likes government in general, because it represents control. Like children, our first reaction is to push against authority, and say "Let me do it myself!" Our particular culture has pushed individualism to extremes, and it is hard to argue for the other side. Still, it's well to ask what are the parameters which could give some reasonable answers to this question of the appropriate role and size of government?

I don't believe this is a matter of conservatives versus progressives, yet there certainly are political and ideological divisions on the question. I'll return to this. But first, notice there is a dilemma built into the very idea of government. If there is not enough social order, then the strong prey on the weak. The weak want to strengthen the law to protect themselves, but when government becomes too overbearing, it is the enemy of both weak and strong. So ordinary people will not have maximum freedom under either a weak or a strong government; it requires a balance. If the elected representatives truly follow the 'will of the people', a strong government may be more acceptable to ordinary people, if they don't care about being dependent – i.e. 'free'.

I personally believe most people don't think clearly about freedom anyway, although they talk about it heatedly. In my experience, what people call 'freedom' is really the ability to do what they wish, which means, to get pleasure and avoid pain. As often as not, people make foolish choices, hoping for pleasure, and end up suffering in the long run. It takes practice to be mature, and immature people aren't free. But government – specifically federal government – control is obviously needed in a number of functions of society. Here are some examples.

National defense
Defense is the first and most obvious obligation of central government. We've already looked at this, and Eisenhower's warning

that the military forces tend to grow, largely because of the economic benefits such growth can bring to states which house the bases, and the industries that get military contracts. Progressives would rather see this money put to national social programs. Conservatives emphasize the business opportunities. Many people think the United States should not wield so much direct military power in the world, and that our foreign policies would be better served with more international cooperation, sharing both defense burdens and trade relations in a less aggressive form. In any case, it seems that military activity around the world is changing to more widespread and less intensive combat, especially in the form of civil wars and terrorism, which require more men, more training, and fewer mass weapon systems. Rather than pretending to know what portion of the central government should go to military defense, I would only suggest that Congress needs to make a much more objective evaluation of priorities. That won't happen until the activities of the government are much more transparent than at present.

Protection against internal threats

Federal laws and law enforcement are needed – strange as it may sound – to protect against insurrections and civil wars. States have tried to secede in the past, individually and in groups, and this is not inconceivable at present. When regional or state-wide characteristics become different enough, with regard to social or economic policies, they can come to uprisings or civil violence, such as occurred in the 'Fifties' and 'Sixties', and still exists in some secessionist movements even today.

Relatedly, particular interest groups come to blows in protest movements such as are seen here regularly, involving perceived injustices in race relations, immigration, unemployment, gender equality, religious freedom, and privacy. Most of these involve 'civil rights' in some form, so they are questions for national policy and implementation.

Money matters

The Treasury is required to manage nation-wide currency creation and distribution, taxation, monetary policies, and international money exchanges. It is inconceivable that the U.S. financial markets should break down into individual state or regional systems, independent of each other or the federal oversight. We will look closely at the nature of money and its connection to the central government in the next chapter.

"And so forth "

The list of activities in which national government has an appropriate place is long and varies over time according to public attitudes and political interests. The point is just to bring the value of national government back into perspective. Names of federal agencies and departments change and subdivide according to their complexity and their perceived importance. It isn't to the point to comment in detail about all of these functions, or others I might add to the list, which are properly the business of central authority. If quizzed, ordinary citizens will admit the need of these just mentioned, and others, such as the use of federal lands, and national parks; food and drug standards; interstate and international trade and tariff questions; efficient and safe transportation, travel and communication, and the infrastructures to support them. And certainly we must include international relations – peaceful and militant – which get so much public attention.

All these activities – regardless of their names, or the size of the agencies involved – were recognized and included in the Constitution from the start, either explicitly or implicitly. Yet it seems that so-called conservative politics – or at any rate as it is expressed publicly in the popular media – keeps up a steady campaign of what looks like a disrespect or even hatred of the national government. It's just "too big", and stifles private business. (Paradoxically, political progressives also seem to dislike government intervention, when it comes to matters of personal lifestyle.) Chapter 8 below will discuss some of the more controversial issues about what kinds of activities are appropriate for government to perform, especially at the national level. But before that, we need to consider the possible funding of such activities, which will be better understood when we analyze modern money theory. That is the topic for Chapter 7.

National and international economic stability

An earlier generation of macroeconomists – most notably Keynes – and contemporary thinkers who follow these principles, believe central governments play an essential role in protecting and advancing the economy. Especially today, it is universally accepted among developed nations that a sovereign currency, not 'pegged' to another currency or tied to any precious metal, gives the greatest freedom to a government to play its crucial part in the economy. The chief role of federal fiscal policies should be to make a 'public sector' contribution to the economy when the 'private sector' contribution is going through one of its periodic downturns; while during periods that are too heated and speculative, it should apply policies and taxation that cool the system, before it blows up. Without these 'counter-cyclical' policies, the economy will go into wild and extreme fluctuations, which are most disruptive.

I'm not qualified to judge how 'big' the federal government must be in order to allow for these stabilizing policies, Some MMT macroeconomists say the size of government should be in the range of twenty to fifty percent of GDP, with the current US budget marking the lower end, and France's case marking the higher end of that range. That suggests the US federal government presently has enough fiscal power to insure national economic health. Whether or not appropriate fiscal measures are enacted is a question of political will. And there are always questions of how to allocate resources to the public benefit, which will be contested in the political realm. Some of these questions about public purpose are the subject for the last two chapters.

Chapter Seven

Debt and Modern Money Theory

Money is social

All the kinds of 'pay' discussed in Chapter 2 show clearly the social origins and social significance of debt, and how to pay it off. But today we have 'money,' and from the common viewpoint, all these other, older means of paying off debt and social obligations – whether by a word or token, a gift or service, treasure or land, goods, chattel or slaves – are only of historic interest at best, and at worst irrelevant. Modern people want modern money. Today people say, "Give me the cash." 'Hard currency' is the goal, and the more the better.

When people are pressed to explain a little further, this usually really means they want the money to buy things they need, like food, clothing and shelter, and some of what they desire, like entertainment and travel, with enough set aside to live comfortably after they retire; and perhaps leave something for their children. They are not misers who simply want the wealth for its own sake, although sadly, that appears to be the motivation controlling financial markets today.

This common view of money is a simple picture, of course – too simple. Most importantly, it leaves out the social meaning of life. Possessions are nice, but not enough to satisfy. It's easy to forget, for example, that we all want to live in communities. We like the services and the interests of a wide variety of people. We count on the friendship and familiarity that neighbors provide. We need parks, attractive surroundings, clean streets and highways that are safe to travel and uncluttered with bill boards. We expect air and water and food to be unpolluted. We count on education, and cultural events and a sense of belonging. And much talked about, we want police protection, security from enemies, and support in times of disaster. Some expect this; others demand it; and still others only hope for it. In brief, aside from our own 'income,' everyone wants a legal, economic and technological environment that provides for convenience, health, and opportunities for personal growth, free self-expression, and useful work that benefits others.[126]

We should keep two points in mind here. The first is rather obvious: the social relationships are what matter to us, even when we're looking for money. Life isn't about owning; it's about *owing*, which is to say, it's about debt in its various forms (which includes "ought" as well as "owe.") It's about all these social interactions and the indebtedness they entail, some of which are good, and some not. The second point is not so obvious. It's true that most of the social relationships that engage us involve, or are 'lubricated' by money – "money makes the world go 'round" – but I want to show that the money itself, for which we so energetically strive, is social too – i.e. social debt.

Money is a debt relation – not a thing

In keeping with the theme of this essay, I want to underscore the idea that *money is debt.* It is not a 'thing', but a relationship – a social relationship, as we have said.[127] When someone gets her first job, whether with a parent or uncle or local business owner, she agrees to do some work for pay, such as babysit, mow the lawn, clean the garage, wash cars, read to Great Auntie Martha, or serve fast food. In my case, my father promised me some money in exchange for doing yard work and weeding the gardens. It was an exchange of debts – what we agreed to owe each other. And so it starts. The need and desire for money grows, along with the skills to earn it. In the process people are introduced to various forms of this 'medium of exchange.' For instance, instead of dealing only in cash, they may decide it's more convenient and safer to be paid by check, which can be deposited directly into a bank account – something that makes children feel 'grown up' – and to withdraw what is needed, and hopefully build up a 'savings account' for future use.

Furthermore, we know that 'cash' isn't always needed for everyday transactions. Most Americans are used to the idea that we can be paid by direct deposit, and pay by automatic withdrawal, by debit or credit cards, and even by 'applications' on our smart phones. And typically for big purchases, like a car, or a house, we can get a loan, and pay that back over time. But many people think that ultimately, all these forms of borrowing somehow go back to cash, dollar bills – i.e. 'currency.' How does this work? Where does the cash come from? And what is it?

Records, 'money of account' and 'money things'

When I work for money, my employer deposits a 'paycheck' into my account. Well, not exactly. My bank credits my account for the amount of the check, and simultaneously debits the employer's account. It's a matter of computer 'keystrokes,' which is to say recording who owes what to whom. If my employer's bank is different from mine, it's just a bit more accounting, to 'clear' his bank's account with my bank. The effect is the same. It's the same if I write checks on my account, or if I use a debit card; my account gets a debit, and the person I pay gets a credit. More record keeping with more key strokes. If I use a credit card, the issuing bank does the same debiting of my account when I use it, and crediting the account of the company where I made my purchase; and they credit my account when I send my Visa or MasterCard issuer a check, or make a 'direct deposit'.[128]

Every credit to my account is a debit to another account, and every debit to my account is a credit to another. The 'money' I have is a measure of the value of that account. If more money is owed to me than I owe to others, I have a positive 'balance.' If I want to buy something, my account balance tells me what buying power I may have for some transaction. The value of my various accounts is measured in US Dollars. That is the "money of account" in this country. It isn't money, but a *standard* for *measuring* money, just as Fahrenheit and Centigrade are standards for measuring temperature. Water boils at 212 degrees Fahrenheit, which equals 100 degrees Centigrade. By whichever standard one uses, the water temperature is the same. And my wealth (or poverty) is the same, whether it's measured in US Dollars, Eropean *Euros* or Brazilian *Reais*, or a dozen other 'monies of account'.

Money, then, is a debt or credit; is not a thing. It has no weight, dimensions or mass. It is not material. But people like to think that money is somehow a physical thing. This error is strengthened by the fact that we all think of money in terms of familiar coins and bills of currency, which *are* physical, *and* they are money. Economists call them 'money things.' Some people worry about the durability and solidity of such objects – and "gold bugs" say all our money should be exchangeable for that precious, beautiful metal.

'Money things' take all sorts of forms, but whatever the form, it is a *token* of the money it represents.[129] Bills and coins are tokens, marked with the amount of money they represent. Their value too lies in the value of some account or other. A check is a 'money thing'. An IOU on paper is a money thing. So is a cash register receipt, or a credit-card transaction slip. Although a bit less material, the computer records of "keystrokes" at the bank are also money things.

Currency

But what about cash? Suppose I do need some money in my pocket – some "dollars" – What is that, and where does it come from? If I withdraw cash from an ATM or bank (my local bank or any other), what am I holding? The bills I put into my wallet – the 'money things' – are very like IOUs, just as are all the tokens of other transactions we have described (check writing, savings deposit, debit and credit card transactions, etc.), passing among the various banking institutions, involving keystrokes and record keeping.

My account balances, and the cash I get, are both measured in the same 'money of account' (i.e. US Dollars) But the cash – the governmental 'IOUs' – are not the same as my pay check. The latter can vary in value, and won't be accepted as payment by just anyone. The bills of US currency have fixed value, and they work the same for anyone who holds the bill. Anyone on the street will recognize their value in a transaction, so they don't require the complicated identification and accounting that banks and private accounts need. They're guaranteed negotiable, unless they are counterfeit. (I wonder why English borrowed the word 'counterfeit' from French.)

When I say the bills or 'notes' of currency, and coins, have fixed value, I mean it is fixed in terms of the 'money of account,' for purposes of keeping records. It remains always the same. A hundred-dollar bill will always be worth a hundred dollars, unless US Government is overthrown, with its Treasury Department. But the value in terms of what the currency notes can buy, or how they relate to other countries' currency, can vary daily, as we know. This is a good place to emphasize another point. When I say that money is all about debt (or credit), it doesn't mean that *'wealth'* is only about the money balances of people's various accounts. Besides money, a person's wealth also includes material goods and property. If she owns a car or house or furniture outright, material property may be a large portion of her total wealth (or 'net worth'). This is especially true of poorer people, whose 'money' wealth is typically very limited, or even negative (for example if they owe a lot on a medical bill, or car loan, or rent), as is more and more the case in recent times.

Wealthy people, by contrast, may own a great deal of property, or material wealth. But still, their total wealth or net worth lies much more in their money or debt wealth – i.e. the positive account balances they have – rather than in material wealth. After all, there is a practical limit to how many possessions one can have, but there is no practical limit to how much money. Whether or not they could ever actually convert this money into a mountain of cash is a moot question. No wealthy person does that. What good would the cash do, except occasionally to help transact illegal business, or escape to another country?

One source of money/ several sources of currency

Where does the currency come from, which customers get at the local bank or ATM? Banks keeps a supply on hand for people who prefer 'cash transactions', and if a bank runs low, it gets resupplied from the Federal Reserve System, through one of the twelve regional Federal Reserve banks, whose accounts are coordinated. That is to say, a bank's 'reserves' at the local Federal bank are debited in exchange for the cash it receives to cover its needs. The paper currency (i.e. the notes, which are 'money things') are shipped to the regional Federal Reserve banks directly from where it is produced (i.e. The Bureau of Printing and Engraving, in D.C. or Fort Worth.) Coins come from one of the four US Mints around the country (which are under the Treasury Department.)[130]

Counter to what old films seemed to imply, ordinary banks don't typically have 'vaults' full of money that customers have previously deposited. In fact, very few customers deposit cash in banks, so there is a lot more cash flowing out to, rather than flowing in from customers. The private banks keep enough cash on hand to meet ordinary needs of their customers, who come there, or go to a local

ATM. If a private bank's customers think their money is not safe, though, or is losing worth, they may make a 'run' on the bank to withdraw their funds in the form of cash; this action can be contagious and cause panic. The "Fed" protects against this by backing up the private bank's reserves with its "high powered money" (HPM) as it's called, and also by guaranteeing a portion of the customer's holdings with a federal insurance policy (FDIC).[131] But if a bank is not economically viable (i.e. it is "insolvent"), it can fail. That decision must be made at the federal level. Today some banks are judged "Too Big To Fail", which causes major problems to the real economy, and benefits only those in the FIRE sector.

"Taxes drive money"

Cash is sometimes described as an 'IOU' because it is a token of debt, like a check, a deposit receipt, or a written IOU, but indirectly. Currency (Federal Reserve notes) all bear the following statement: "This note is legal tender for all debts, public and private." ('Tender' is a legal document that one 'tenders' to another, as in "I tendered my resignation".) The sentence printed on the note is not a *description*, but *a prescription*; it is a statement of law. However, when the national government puts notes ('money') into circulation, it says that they *can* be used to pay any debt, but not that they *must* be. In some societies, and at times in our past history, people have not trusted the government issued currency, and have refused to accept it. Even where "legal tender laws" are written, people may still refuse.

What makes US currency generally accepted for ordinary transactions today is the fact that the federal government insists that it must be used for payment of any debt *to the government itself* – in particular for *tax* payment. It will only accept payments in its own currency. Since every citizen and business has to keep a certain amount of the government's money on hand to pay taxes, there is great incentive to use it for all debts (i.e. all transactions), both public and private. To refuse to use it would be very inconvenient for the refusing party, and she might also be subject to legal action by others with whom she deals, who expect payment in US currency.

A $100 bill (note) is no more valuable or real as money than a $100 check, although it is certainly more trustworthy. After all, the check may be falsified, or drawn on an account that has no funds, or one that has been closed. We say the currency money is 'fungible' because it can circulate immediately, and go freely among citizens. US currency is guaranteed to be accepted by the federal government, and it can be passed around in payment for private transactions, with the confidence that it is 'good'. It doesn't name the holder; its value is marked on it; and it has no expiration date. (Again, we see the importance of social relationships in money matters.) The government will credit any payment the holder makes to the government, using its own currency – e.g. to pay a fine, or an entry fee into a national park, and especially to pay any taxes. Other, non-governmental agencies, public and private, will similarly credit payments in the same currency, unless they are foolish.

In effect, currency notes are IOUs – i.e. tokens of credit for taxes, or any other financial obligations payable to the government. It is also a 'debt against the government', in the sense of an obligation to accept it in payment. The central government 'owes' the holder of the note the amount of credit for the amount on the note, in payment of any federal debt. If the term 'IOU' is not clear in this context, use the word 'credit;' the practical effect is the same. [132] Here are some analogies. Many restaurants issue gift cards of a specified value, without a name written on them, which they will honor, no matter who presents them. These cards could act as 'money' among friends, in a limited way, since the card holders are confident that the issuing restaurants will ultimately 'redeem' them (for a restaurant meal).

Another analogy is the strings of 'tickets' which are printed for use in festivals and fairs, to purchase food or drinks or other items. So long as you're on the fairgrounds, they are valid, and can be used for purchases, and are often exchanged among visitors: ("I'll give you ten tickets for that cup of beer.") But outside the grounds, or after the fair, whatever extra tickets you're still holding are useless, and represent a waste of money.

A third illustrative example would be a person who holds an IOU from another person, and uses that IOU to pay off a debt that she owes to a third party. If Kay gave me her IOU in exchange for $100 cash she borrowed, and marked it 'payable on demand to the holder', I can use her IOU to pay a bill at my corner store, but only if the store owner is willing to accept it. In that case, Kay's debt to me has become Kay's debt to the store owner. That means that the 'liability' is transferable, or 'negotiable'. Dan Kervick makes this 'third party debt' understandable in a recent article: "Do Banks Create Money from Thin Air?"[133]

These examples illustrate, in a sense, that money (i.e. debt) can be created, when one issues an IOU, and also why currency can be looked on as an IOU, or a 'negotiable liability' on the government. Anyone can issue an IOU. If it is accepted and negotiable, it becomes money. This is what commercial banks do in effect when they issue loans: they 'lend money into existence;' and it's what the Federal bank does when it spends money that the Treasury department has authorized. It 'spends money into existence'. In both cases, the money comes into existence from nothing previous, just like the IOU. But there is a big difference. The private banks' loans are against "reserves" they have in the federal reserve system, so they have the backing of the government money. All of these forms of debt or 'liabilities' are negotiable. Keeping them that way is the function of the banking systems at both the private and public level.

But ultimately, it is the Treasury Department, through the Fed, that 'creates' the money. The systems are authorized, supervised and adjusted by law, and supported by the confidence of those who use them. As the often-quoted economist Hyman Minsky suggested, "Anyone can create money. The problem is getting it accepted." [134]

Once again, we see that debt is a function of social relationships – in this case the societal decisions of the national government – presumably made for the benefit of the citizens it represents.

Gold standard

Today one hears a lot of political talk, suggesting that the United States' money is 'weak', because gold no longer 'backs' the currency. There are those who advocate return to precious metals, derisively called "gold bugs" by their opponents[135] Gold backing causes problems. Britain went off the gold standard in 1931, in an effort to increase their money supply and encourage growth after the depression. It was a good move; gold-backed currency was holding them back – i.e. keeping them from meeting the need for more money to stimulate the economy. They needed 'liquidity'. After WWII, in the 1944 Bretton Woods agreement, Britain (somewhat reluctantly)[136] and other nations within the sphere of American economic growth, established a "gold exchange" standard. This meant that a foreign central bank could (with some restrictions) exchange US currency for gold bullion to adjust their currency's value. Note that individual citizens did not have this power. Most of these economies were "floating" – i.e. their currency was adjusted to stay in sync with the US Dollar, which was the dominant currency, and still is. However, setting the value of the US Dollar at $35 dollars per ounce continued to limit the flexibility of US monetary policies, as well as those economies that were tied to the US Dollar.

Even previously, under various gold standards, the money's value was never really determined by the value of the gold backing; it was the other way around. The government said how 'valuable' the gold was by setting its price at a fixed rate. An added problem was that collaborating governments could 'trade in' their US Dollar reserves for gold. France did this, and the results of that 'hit', together with other problems for the U.S. – especially the costs of the war in

Vietnam – motivated the US government to let go of the 'exchange' part of the system in 1971, under President Nixon. After a few inadequate adjustments of the 'price' of gold, the standard was abandoned altogether in 1976 (the Bicentennial year for America), when Congress omitted all laws and references to gold on the currency, and the Dollar was allowed to 'float' freely.[137]

Although the question of gold backing is politically controversial today, economically it is not. Historical research suggests that a gold standard was always problematic. Even in the long history of the use of gold (or silver) coins as currency, there were always problems of 'liquidity' – i.e. keeping enough money in circulation. The value of coins was set by governmental degree – not by some natural or market value of gold (or silver) as a 'commodity'. This further argues for the claim that all debt is ultimately a social matter; even the value of money debt is determined by governmental laws, which are social and only social. Christine Desan of Harvard has given a critique of the 'mythology' of gold as 'money' in her study "Coin Reconsidered". She summarizes her findings, thus:

> Medieval coin plays an essential role in the *imagined* history of money: it figures as the primal "commodity money" – a natural medium, spontaneously adopted by parties in exchange who converge upon a metal like silver to represent the value of other goods... But as the history offered here reveals, medieval money was nothing like its imagined alternative. England's early coin became a medium when the government began to spend and tax in that unit of account, took coin as a mode of payment, and allowed it to be transferred between people in the meantime. Individuals participated in the arrangement, paying for coin in exchange for the unique quality – liquidity – that set money apart from a commodity. . . [I]nsofar as the English equated money with the commodity it contained, they engineered instability into the heart of their medium. Depreciating coin – diluting its

commodity content – offered a cure. It also confirmed that coin had never been the "commodity money" imagined in later accounts. Coin was, instead, a constitutional medium, one that related the government to its participants and thus helped to configure the world it appeared merely to measure.[138]

In today's economy, when gold is no longer needed, even the 'unbacked currency' itself does not ultimately 'support' the economy. That is easy to see simply from the fact that all the US currency, in this nation and around the world, amounts to slightly over one trillion dollars ($1 trillion), whereas US total annual economic output alone – private, public and international – is many times that amount (about $16 trillion in 2012).[139]

Look at any bill again. It reads, "This note is legal tender for all debts, public and private". That's all, but in the case of a solvent and sovereign state, that's enough. What is it that 'backs up' the Federal bank's currency? "The full faith and credit" of the nation, or what is the same, the belief that the creativity, economic energy and future development of the nation can be counted on. Once again, these are social relationships. The money and the economy depend on them, and not the other way around.

Sovereign currency

A "sovereign currency" is one whose creation is at the discretion of a government, and is not determined by outside political forces. Of course, the 'value' of that currency (in terms of its purchasing power) will depend on the market in which it is used, which means on the judgment of the people who use it. A government may try to force its people to use currency, but the attitudes of the citizens, together with their connection to other 'markets' – e.g. Cuban family members in other countries – will affect the value greatly. Cubans are paid very low wages by their dictatorial government, and prices of basic goods are controlled as well. So the Cuban Peso has 'worth' – it can buy needed goods – but the normal wages received won't cover basic needs, let alone luxuries priced according to international standards. People try desperately to get 'tourist dollars', in order to make ends meet. So even sovereign money won't solve problems without coordinating with other trade partners.

Most nations in the world, including the U.S., let their currencies 'float' – i.e. their value is determined by a "foreign exchange market" that fluctuates from day to day. At present, the US Dollar is the most popular currency, but there are others, like the *Euro*, the *Yen*, the *Pound*, the Norwegian *Krone*, the Swiss *Franc*, and the Canadian and Australian Dollars. The Chinese *Renminbi* is still a minor influence in the currency market (less than 1% as of 2012).[140] All of these currencies are said to be "sovereign". This is an extremely important point to keep in mind, when one is considering the political discussions centering on "fiscal policy", such as those which moved me to write this essay.

An example of currency that is not sovereign is the *Euro* today. Each of the Euro zone countries is bound to use the common currency, which is in the hands of the European Central Bank (ECB). Therefore, the fiscal policies of each Euro zone nation depend on decisions about the currency that are beyond their legislators' control. Since each nation has its particular set of economic problems, this arrangement ties the fiscal hands of individual governments. One can see the unhappy results of this fact, for example, in the "austerity" measures which have left Greece, Spain, Portugal, Italy and Ireland in a condition of massive unemployment and hardship, and have put a wet blanket over the European economy generally. The point is, a "sovereign" currency allows its government the greatest flexibility to decide what economic policies to follow, and which fiscal programs it can implement to the greatest benefit. These do not depend on 'affordability' or 'national debt', as I shall try to show.

'Sectors' of the economy

It seems useful to emphasize "macroeconomics" here and especially in the next two sections. Ideas that come from looking at the economy in the biggest picture – in the 'aggregate' as it is said – sometimes may contradict those we are used to holding in our day-to-day view of money business. The first is that our economic system can be considered as a whole, and in a sense analyzed as a 'closed system'. We all know that communications, and travel, and business relationships (all 'social,' remember) make it feel that the only 'unity' we could imagine is the entire world, which is far too complex to understand systematically. But, in economic terms, it can be simplified, to make a clearer picture.

The first thing to remember is that economists talk in generalities such as GDP, and GNP, and lump into those terms only the kinds of things and activities that can be given a dollar value. These are not precise numbers, but are close enough to see trends, and to make reasonable decisions about business and government policies. Secondly, although businesses of all sorts have trends and flows that change from moment to moment, accountants can nevertheless make end of year statements about liabilities and assets, even though the final accounting is not in. (How can the bank know whether I will miss a payment, or default on a loan, or negotiate a change in interest rate, when it calls my mortgage an asset and gives it a value?)

Third, and most important, the numbers only count 'balances' – i.e. the sum of assets and liabilities (resulting from credits and debits) – in terms of money. They don't reflect personal possessions, or care that a farm has been in the family for four generations, or who is a laborer and who an artist, or how hard people work and whether they feel fulfilled, or what is harming the environment, or how attractive the neighborhood is, or how healthy or safe the citizens are, or what is their level of education or divorce rate, except in-so-far as all these relate to some money accounting. (Needless to say, most of them do involve money, in one way or another.)

We can simplify any national economy into 'sectors' in various ways – e.g. the 'private sector' (including households and businesses) and the 'public sector' (including all branches of government, like police, town councils, schools, state medical programs, military defense, etc).We know that every liability of one party represents an equal asset of another party, so that the sum total of liabilities and assets is zero, in money terms. If the Private Sector as a whole accumulates net financial *assets*, the Public Sector *must* accumulate net financial *liabilities* of the same amount.The sectors balance.

But a two-sector model is too simple, because we also need to think about foreign business, especially exports and imports. It is more realistic and helpful to add a third sector – call it the 'Everything Else' or Foreign Sector. The basic point to keep in mind is that the balances of all these sectors – their net financial assets and liabilities – must add up to zero. In other terms, budget *surpluses* must match budget *deficits,* for the accounting to make logical sense. In the Private Sector, the balance may be positive, if the assets are greater than the liabilities, or negative. Similarly, in the Public Sector, the balance may be positive or negative. And similarly, in the Foreign (or trade) Sector, the balance may be positive, or negative. But the *net* financial assets of all three sectors added together *must be zero*. It's impossible for these three balances to be either all positive, or all negative. The graph that follows gives a picture of what this means.[141]

In this graph, Matthew Berg has used the labels "Domestic Private Sector Balance," "Government Balance" and "Capital Account" instead of 'Private Sector', 'Public Sector,' and 'Foreign Sector' but for practical purposes they mean the same, and show what is important. The numbers represent the 'percentages of GDP' of those sectors, at the times shown; it doesn't show the general growth of GDP. The numbers given represent 'net financial assets' on the top of the graph, and 'net financial liabilities' on the bottom; we can see they are exact mirror images. In other words, the sum of these sector balances above and below the line is always zero, as we said.

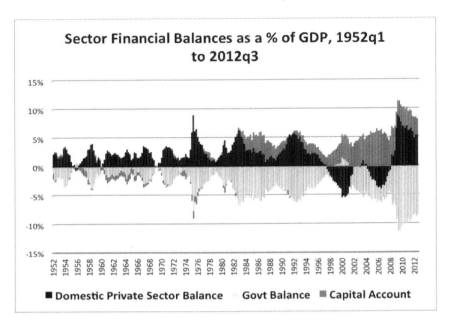

The chart spans sixty years of ups and downs in the US economy's history. Most recently, we can see the collapses of the so-called Dot Com and Housing bubbles (2001 and 2007, respectively). Notice the little blip of light gray 1999 to 2001, when the government ran a positive balance at the end of the Clinton presidency. It was a strange period, when people went into debt by investing in property and stocks, thinking they were wealthy, because they counted their nominal 'market value' holdings (e.g. property and stocks) as real wealth. This fueled the housing bubble and collapse, and brought on the GFC (Global Financial Crisis) and recession that followed. The thing to keep in mind here, by way of understanding, is that for one sector to have a surplus, some other sector must have a deficit. Whether that deficit should be in the Foreign, Private, or Public Sector is a question for political discourse and fiscal policy decisions.

Typically, the US 'trade balance' is negative, and has been so for many years. That is to say, the Foreign Sector ('the rest of the world') has a positive balance, which means that money is, on net, leaving the US economy; it isn't coming into it. It follows from this simple equation, that if the Foreign Sector is making money (its balance is positive), and the Public Sector runs a balanced budget (i.e. net financial assets are zero) or is positive (i.e. it is 'saving'), then the Private Sector must be *in deficit* (i.e. households owe more than they have; and/or businesses are going further into debt. On the other hand, if the Private Sector (households and businesses) want to 'make money' (i.e. run a surplus), then the Public Sector *has* to 'lose money' (i.e. run deficits budgets, and increase debt). We can't 'have it both ways'. So long as the 'rest of the world' has a positive balance against the U.S., it's impossible to accumulate assets in the private part of the economy (households and businesses), without having a deficit in the governmental agencies of the economy (which can be federal, state or local).

Many countries do run a positive trade balance. They export more than they import. China has been that way for a long period. For them it is possible for the private sector to make money without the public sector going into debt, but at present that is not the condition for the U.S. There are arguments for and against our becoming a nation of exporters, but that goes beyond the purpose and scope of this essay. In any case, it is irrelevant to our present state of affairs; the U.S. will probably be a net importer for a long time to come. We are stuck with trying to balance the private sector with the public sector.

"Paradox of thrift," austerity, spending and deflation

In the present recession conditions, government authorities of both political parties, both houses of Congress, and the Executive branch have been pushing for 'austerity', at least in the media. That is, "Don't spend more than you make" (or what is equivalent, "Don't pass deficit budgets"). From a macroeconomic perspective, however, this makes no sense. To 'balance the budget', their efforts are to increase taxes, or to decrease governmental expenses or both at the same time. (President Obama calls the effort a "Great Bargain," while his critics call it a "Great Betrayal".) The general public seems to have accepted the idea of austerity, reluctantly, but their versions of it depend on their views of whose taxes and which public programs should be considered for 'adjustment'. However, it can be shown that in macroeconomic terms, austerity, or 'thrift', is *not a virtue*. This "paradox of thrift" is very counterintuitive, and controversial, for it seems to oppose moral and religious habits of thought that are deeply (and properly) entrenched in our value set.

J. M. Keynes explained the "paradox of thrift" as an example of the Fallacy of Composition in 1936, during the Great Depression.[142] Such a fallacy is to think that whatever is true of the parts of a whole must also be true of the whole. Not necessarily so. For example, if all the parts of a car are expensive, then the car is expensive (which is true); or, if every hour of a day lasts sixty minutes, then the day lasts sixty minutes (which is false); or, if all the students in a school are old, then the school is old (which may be true or false); or if all the members of a group are fat, then the group is fat (which makes no sense). The point of the fallacy then is, it's not logically safe to say that what is true of parts must be true of the whole.

Applying this thinking to national economies as a whole, it's *not* true that 'thrift' or 'austerity' is always good policy. The error is to think that thrift is good for each member of the society, so it must be good for the society as a whole, 'in the aggregate'. Why is this false? Because typically a nation's economy develops when its citizens work to earn money for expenses, and businesses produce goods to sell to those earners. When one person is 'thrifty' – i.e. she saves by cutting back on expenses – her action has little large-scale effect. But if everyone cuts back, then businesses will lose sales and let go of employees, employees will have to cut back even further, and a vicious cycle begins. That is called "deflation". We're in it now.

Another paradoxical difference between the macroeconomic and the personal level of economics has to do with how spending and income are related. In the lives of individual citizens, spending habits are pretty well determined by income. It is safe to say that as people's incomes increase or decrease, so will their spending increase or decrease. However, at the macroeconomic or 'aggregate' level, it seems to be the other way around. An increase of aggregate *spending* brings about an increase in aggregate *income*.[143] This is why there is so much talk in the media about 'consumer confidence' and other measures of growth in spending.

In so-called developed nations, which are 'socially progressive', there are laws in place which work to offset problems that citizens have in the ordinary course of their lives, because of loss of employment, injury, medical emergencies, natural disasters, retirement, the relocation of an industry out of a community, etc. So it is logical to expect the public sector to contribute more than ordinarily to the economy when the economy is in a general recession – i.e. when the private sector is pulling back. And that is what does happen, as the 'sector balance' equations show over time, as described above.

The only group of citizens who may benefit from 'austerity' in the long run are those, mentioned earlier, whose incomes are increased by lowering wages, which will occur if the public sector 'safety net' programs are reduced or eliminated (like social security, workmen's compensation, minimum wage laws, disability pensions, unemployment insurance, job placement programs, food stamps and the like). These cuts will encourage employees to work more for less. This is especially helpful to the 'rentier' class, which benefits most from the profitability of the enterprises it owns; it has little to lose from high unemployment. It appears from media accounts that this group also might accept higher taxes, which seems strange. However, that 'compromise' probably comes from the realization that tax increases will fall most heavily not on those at the top ('The 1/10th of 1%'), but on those nearer the middle of the income scale. Moreover, capital gains, bond holdings and other investments are typical sources of wealth in this class, which are taxed at lower rates than ordinary income. We discussed this above in the chapter on oligarchy.

In a recession, people are already being let go, and their incomes are reduced. To compound the situation, local and state governments cut back programs and raise tax rates, in the effort to 'conserve' resources. But reducing wages also reduces tax revenues, and often the whole process begins to move in a 'deflationary cycle', with unhappy results, both social and economic. Keynes pointed out that in recessionary periods, the public sector (government) should, and typically does, put money into the economy, to offset the slump in the private sector. This is what 'stimulus' is about. Keep in mind that local and state governments are not able to do the stimulating, because of their reduced tax revenues and increased burdens of providing a 'safety net' for the underemployed and unemployed. So it is left to the central government to make up the slack in the private sector economy. People who worry that 'stimulus spending' might result in inflation should realize that *deflation* is a much graver prospect than inflation in the conditions of recession seen today, and is harder to escape once it begins.

Keynes was not simply an advocate of big government however – although his enemies still try to encourage this myth. He said, for example, "[T]he boom, not the slump, is the right time for austerity of the Treasury."[144] He did not say that austerity is never a good idea. Keynes' effort was to develop "counter-cyclical" responses to fluctuations in the economy. Instability, and wide swings up and down are the things to avoid, if possible. To accomplish counter cyclical policies, the central government must have sufficient 'economic power'. I don't know what that would mean in terms of percentage of GDP. Among the developed nations, as mentioned previously, France lies at the higher end, with the Public Sector at about fifty percent of GDP; while the U.S. lies at the lower end, with about twenty percent. Conservatives tend to say that is too much.

National debt and inflation

One last idea about modern money applies to the current angry public rhetoric, and fiscal policy decisions about "national debt". The gross national debt has steadily increased in the past thirty-five years, from $1 trillion before Reagan to $16.4 trillion today. Critics of continued growth in the national debt (called 'deficit hawks' by their opponents) agree with House Speaker John Boehner that "our government has built up too much debt. ... At $16 trillion and rising, our national debt is draining free enterprise and weakening the ship of state". (Jan 3, 2013) In fact, the current law requires setting a 'ceiling' to debt, which is frequently raised. 'Crises' occur regularly, when Congress threatens to 'shut down' government, rather than extend the debt limit.

Common sense would suggest that this ever-increasing debt is a bad idea, or even a 'ticking time bomb', and that eventually the 'chickens will come home to roost,,' or 'the piper must be paid', or 'the Devil will come to collect the soul' of the nation, or some such metaphor. However, as said earlier, sometimes common sense simply is mistaken in issues of macroeconomics, or the nation as a whole.

Advocates of so-called "Modern Money Theory" (MMT) have an uphill battle to get their ideas into the mainstream discussion of economic policies, which presently follow an orthodox view initiated by people like Milton Friedman[145] (of the Chicago School), and Ludwig Von Mises and Friedrich Hayek (of the Austrian School). Generally they opposed any governmental interference in the economy. But there are those who have begun to reconsider, such as Kenneth Newman, a deputy secretary of the Treasury in the Clinton Administration:

America has convinced itself that it can no longer afford many of the productive things that it has done so well over its history. Infrastructure repair, jobs programs, military modernization, tax reduction...have all been stifled because of this fear.[146]

The fear is a fear of debt, which is both a moral view that debt is somehow wrong in and of itself (a strange perspective, since debt is the basis of capitalism), as well as a fear of the expected consequences of debt – primarily of inflation. But the first question to ask is what this national debt means, and by whom and to whom is it owed? We've already emphasized that the Treasury can 'spend money into existence', whenever it authorizes contracts for various goods and services at the behest of the US government. It then indirectly credits the accounts of the providers of those goods and services by increasing the 'reserves' at the Federal Reserve system which become available to private banks, who will serve the capital and operating needs of those contractors.

This federal money is not taken from a pre-existent source provided by taxes, or other payments to the government. It is 'created by key strokes', as explained earlier. So the government cannot default, i.e. it cannot go beyond its ability to pay for the obligations it has put on itself. However, since the idea of budgeting suggests there is some limit to the funding, the public (and its politician representatives) talk heatedly about spending beyond its means.

It is of course possible for the government to spend more than it *should* at any particular time – an evaluation that depends on judgments about what is needed at that time. It should not be determined relative to a certain fixed number that might be called the budget 'surplus' or 'deficit', or in the long run, a zero-point in so-called national debt. "Too much" or "too little" spending are properly determined by the present conditions of the economy. If the economic machinery is working at capacity, and everyone is employed, then adding government expenses to the system would indeed be harmfully inflationary. On the other hand, when the private sector is stagnant, or in contraction, and/or when there are tens of millions of unemployed citizens (as is presently the case, and most likely will continue for a long time), then government spending is needed. The restrictions should be determined by democratic decisions about which projects and programs are most useful for the public good.

Inflation can be managed in various ways by governmental policies. Generally, taxes can put a damper on an overheated economy. This is their primary monetary purpose. Taxes are not to 'earn enough' to pay for governmental needs. In addition, the Fed can set its interest rate 'targets' at whatever point will avoid inflation, and the money supply will adjust. When Treasury bonds are sold, it is not because the government needs to borrow, but because it wants to affect the money supply. So long as the interest rates do not exceed the growth rate of GDP, government spending and some consequent inflation are not harmful; indeed, they are a sign of a developing, healthy economy.

Finally, we might mention that there are two parts of the so-called national debt. One part is where some individual federal agency has gone over its budget limit, and so it 'borrows' funds from another federal agency (like "robbing Peter to pay Paul"). Therefore, the effective debt (the part 'owed' to the public) is only about two thirds of the nominal total debt – at present about $11 trillion.

To summarize then, it is possible to reframe the discussion about debt, and to change the way it is perceived. Since the word 'debt' itself is inherently negative in its connotations, and since the central government with a sovereign currency can never default on its obligations to pay, there may be a better 'meme' to use, which more accurately represents the positive role played in the economy by federal spending. Instead of speaking about 'deficit' budgets, and growing 'national debt,' one could simply speak about the 'federal contribution' to the overall economy – which quite properly involves goods and services that the private, money-oriented sector cannot (or will not) provide. But I don't expect the memes or the present angry rhetoric will change any time soon, because they work to the benefit of those who think that maximizing profits is the only realistic way of looking at capitalism, regardless of who is left without a useful job, or the means to participate in the social good, except as passive receivers of so-called welfare.

Chapter Eight

Fiscal Policy and Public Purpose

"Conservative"/ "Libertarian"/ "Liberal"/ "Progressive"

Without talking about 'fairness' of any particular distribution of wealth, or making judgments about the moral character of any particular persons at the top of the wealth scale, we can nevertheless discuss several moral issues – all related – which attach to the current inequality we have been examining.[147]

All the questions of this chapter, as well as the next about education are controversial. Fiscal policies about them on the part of central government necessarily will entail disputes and compromises reflecting the changeable political climate. From some perspectives, the questions should not even be discussed as matters for fiscal policy decisions at the national level; they are matters for private individuals and/or local governments it is said. From other perspectives, they involve aspects of a good society, and suggest what government should aim at, when it constructs its fiscal policies.

Power over lawmaking

We spoke above of the historic disagreements at the inception of this country regarding how to divide the power of the various parts of government, and how to guard against abuses of either a minority or a majority of citizens which could become dictatorial. For the present discussion about public purpose and fiscal policies, I only wish to emphasize that the distribution of power in the country is not just a matter of legal limits and constitutional structures. In practice, power is wielded, as we have argued, in many legal, extra-legal and illegal ways, so that the first order of improving national wellbeing is always to put power where is should be. That is not easy; and deciding where it should be is disputable.

American citizens pride themselves with the thought that their nation is committed (as Lincoln put it) to "government of the people, by the people, for the people". However, government 'by the people' is indirect, and properly so. Any attempt at *direct democracy* – i.e. where the general public decides issues without agents or intermediaries – would be ridiculous at the national level. If the 'will of the people' which changes from moment to moment were to determine laws, there would obviously be continual chaos.

The issue of popular control of government is really a matter of finding representatives who are genuinely working for the interests of their constituents. This in turn requires ordinary citizens to develop the habit of involving themselves in social issues at all levels, starting locally, and early in life, so that they are aware of what needs doing and how to do it, and know how to find trustworthy representatives, or become such themselves. This was an idea that John Dewey emphasized, at a time of great industrial development, uncontrolled monopolies, influx of immigrants, and international affairs which were putting stress on the country. Political contests were intense.[148]

Dewey thought 'democracy' is a *way of life* – of involvement in society – that people must learn from practice. People who are used to participating, in a serious and influential way (especially in local activities, such as a school council, or a block club, or the town commission on park beautification), will make themselves knowledgeable, because they want others to respect their thoughts. They will rise to the occasion, and have something beneficial to contribute to the conversation.

By contrast with this ideal, the typical political involvement of ordinary citizens today is to ignore local activities, and to concentrate on the 'big' picture, in state and federal politics. Their involvement is sterile, however, because they are remote from the process, as the previous section showed, and subject to hype and deception. They are simply observers of events which are 'spun' and presented in popular media accounts. Although they are deluded into thinking to the contrary, their periodic voting in state and federal elections has no serious effect on policy decisions which influence their daily lives.

Without the sense of involvement spoken of by Dewey, citizens will not make themselves aware of what is really happening in their government. And without that knowledge, lawmakers can work independently and unobserved by their constituents, and often for their own interests. But more important, if constituents are ignorant of what truly is in their own interests – and society's – then they can't hold their representatives to account to enact beneficial policies, presuming their representatives might actually follow constituents' suggestions. To put this briefly, people who 'govern themselves' (which is democracy) cannot do so well unless they understand what is truly to their benefit, and can reasonably trust their representatives to work towards those goals.

Searching for truth v. searching for power

Plato understood these problems of democracy. For his critical insights he has sometimes been called an 'enemy of democracy'.[149] I agree that Plato was not a fan of democracy as he saw it (nor was his student Aristotle.) But I think it's fairer to say he understood that democracy won't work well unless the governed know what is good for them, and are not subject to the manipulation of self-interested demagogues (or today, in a less obvious but more effective way, by self-interested oligarchs who know how to influence public opinion). I'm sure he was right. Others have said democracy is not the best governing system; it's just better than all the others.

In principle, there is nothing wrong with democracy, if it means a group effort to find how best to govern the state. "Two heads are better than one" is true, but only so long as the group is unified in its purpose to solve a problem. This is typically the case with medical research or internet technology, and it could be the case with legislative bodies. Unfortunately, as Plato pointed out, there is a natural (and perhaps inevitable) tendency in democratic forms of government to stop looking for *truth* – i.e. the right way to guide the state – and instead to start looking for *power*. The members of the legislature start trying to benefit themselves or their friends, by whatever means they can use, rather than finding what is best.

Civil rights v. a sense of community

Civil rights are a foundation of western social philosophy, and are built into the constitutional structure of American government. The idea that all citizens are equal under law, and that each has access to the process of lawmaking are fundamental to democracy. It's appropriate, then, that government policies not only protect individuals and minority groups from abuse, but also if needed, to take positive steps (and spend money) to level the field, in some places. This last point, however, is problematic.

For example, if public buildings or buses are made 'handicap accessible', few citizens seem to object, so long as funds are available. It could be argued that it benefits only a small part of a community, but others may say it is a 'public good' to maximize the opportunities for everyone; and besides, any of us might end up in those circumstances. The question is whether public generosity to individual needs can end up hurting the community in the effort to benefit some of its members. Or, putting it another way, a proper balance is needed, between societal good and individual good.

There is no correct answer to what balance is best, much less how to achieve it. Practices differ from culture to culture, and from one time to another. Still, it's clear to me that individualism and narrow self-interest have grown to dominate the thinking of American society, in degrees and ways that are destructive of community. No doubt there are many reasons for this, including the tendencies of unchecked human nature. A big step towards improvement, which is workable but not easy, might be a national campaign to encourage *objectivity* and *civility* in the examination, presentation and solution of problems. Educators, politicians, religious leaders, bureaucrats, non-profit agencies, business organizations, media personalities and householders could join in at no risk. "Have an open mind" is a motto that encourages something people recognize to be a good quality (in principle), and I think to practice and encourage it does not need to be threatening or confrontational.

There is no shortage of 'teachable moments'. But needless to say, I don't expect my proposal to catch on. Too many people benefit from stirring emotion and appealing to prejudice, in market places, legislatures, media centers, news rooms, and pulpits. What could they gain from active listening or civility, and why would they encourage it in others?

Full employment

For a long time, American congresses and administrations, regardless of party, have committed to the value of high employment, and stable prices, as part of their economic plans. However, since the entrenchment of neo-classical economic theory in the last three or four decades among mainstream economists and their associates in government, it's believed that these two goals are incompatible. It is thought that efforts to keep employment high lead to unmanageable price inflation, and policy makers have chosen to choose price stability and deal with unemployment as it happens, either by 'priming the pump' with stimulus programs, or simply by providing public assistance to the unemployed, as needed. These latter social programs have been under increasingly intense criticism by conservative political groups for the past three decades, to the point where just last month, Nobel Prize winning economist Paul Krugman called it "War on the Unemployed" in a *New York Times* editorial.[150] Krugman argues that cuts to unemployment insurance payments in North Carolina and other states and the Federal elimination of the extension of such benefits is "a case of meanspiritedness with bad economic analysis".

> In general, modern conservatives believe that our national character is being sapped by social programs that, in the memorable words of Paul Ryan, the chairman of the House Budget Committee, "turn the safety net into a hammock that lulls able-bodied people to lives of dependency and complacency." More specifically, they believe that unemployment insurance encourages jobless workers to stay unemployed, rather than taking available jobs...
>
> Won't making the unemployed desperate put downward pressure on wages? And won't lower labor costs encourage job growth? No — that's a fallacy of composition. Cutting one worker's wage may help save his or her job by making that worker cheaper than competing workers; but cutting everyone's wages just reduces everyone's income — and it worsens the burden of debt, which is one of the main forces holding the economy back.

Oh, and let's not forget that cutting benefits to the unemployed, many of whom are living hand-to-mouth, will lead to lower overall spending — again, worsening the economic situation, and destroying more jobs.

The move to slash unemployment benefits, then, is counterproductive as well as cruel; it will swell the ranks of the unemployed even as it makes their lives ever more miserable.

Randall Wray and other modern money theorists argue against the economic (and social) theories that support conservative Republican fiscal policies.[151] It is possible, they argue, to have employment that is 'full' – i.e. all people employed who are able and willing – without either competing with the private economy, or producing inflation. To accomplish this desirable goal, Wray advocates public service employment programs. Wray uses the phrase 'public service employment' (PSE) instead of 'employer of last resort' (PLR) which is also used, but sounds demeaning. 'Job Guarantee' (JG) is another name often heard. These programs can be managed either by the federal government directly, or if people prefer, by states, through local government agencies, like school districts, or even by non-governmental agencies and non-profit groups. In any case, the programs are funded by the federal government. The programs will be more or less active as the economy goes through its normal ups and downs, and they will help to moderate the cycles.

PSE workers will not compete with either private sector or public sector employees, whose wages are determined by market trends and labor relations regulation. PSE wages will be set by Congress, and maintained at a level equivalent to a 'living wage' which will be adjusted as needed periodically. Whereas other public and private workers can set their own wages by negotiation, the PSE wage will effectively become the national *minimum wage*, because anyone can fall back on this job guarantee if all else fails.

Any PSE program should include encouraging and training workers to be eligible for work in the private sector, or other freely chosen positions in the public sector which provide higher incentives. Part of PSE work might even be a full-time job search for a limited period. If private employers can hire PSE workers away whenever they are thought to be productive enough to merit higher wages, this will act as a price stabilizing force – not a force for inflation. There are several other economic objections generally raised against such full employment programs, which Wray also answers.

As the PSE program is implemented, there will be an increase in aggregate demand for workers in the private sector too, since the overall demand for goods and services will increase. But this will not increase the deficit, since workers can move from the PSE to the private sector, which will offset the cost to the government by a roughly equivalent amount. What's more, the cost of public services for unemployment will lessen proportionately. This program, then, will not cause so-called 'demand pull' inflation, which is the usual worry of those who oppose job guarantee programs; indeed it can help to stabilize prices.

Another inflationary issue relates to the idea that as aggregate wages increase, supplies of goods will go down because employers cannot afford the more expensive labor to produce them, and this will lead to rising prices; this is the so-called 'cost-push' inflation. It might be thought that because the government is now paying previously unpaid workers, the increase in aggregate labor costs will increase the price of goods. That is true, but only for a one-time jump – not an increasing inflationary cycle.

It might also be thought that because workers realize they can always fall back on the PSE program in a pinch, they will confidently keep making higher wage demands on their employers, which will start an inflationary cycle of higher prices and higher wages. Again, the worry is not realistic, because as private sector wages rise farther above the base PSE wage, which is fixed, employees will be taking a greater and greater risk by demanding still higher wages.

No doubt the PSE program of guaranteed employment will cost money, for wages, for training, and for management and supervision. On the other hand, it will lessen the need for other assistance programs that are designed to help the unemployed. And, as said above, each time the private sector economy improves, the PSE program expenses will diminish, lowering government costs. Such a program will cost something permanently, and in that sense will be a source of low inflation. (Wray estimates the cost of such a program in the United States would be less than one percent of GDP.) But contrary to what conservatives think, with the fiat currency of our system (and the systems of all the other developed nations), a small amount of inflation is actually desirable, because among other things it represents the fact that the economy is growing overall, and the private sector is in the black.

Socially useful work

Two final points can be mentioned in favor of full employment, regardless of its *economic* pros and cons. In the first place, PSE programs can be geared to take care of societal needs which the private sector is historically unwilling, and even unable, to meet, because there is no 'profit' in them; this includes infrastructure and environmental improvement, and social needs, as we will discuss below. These are not 'make work' projects, as their critics often characterize them, but should be designed to serve the society, and the persons who work in them, like WPA during the Depression era.

Secondly, the PSE program represents a commitment to the importance of work. Although some cynics might feel that labor is only undertaken out of necessity, and to earn one's living, I believe it is part of what being human entails – not specifically the wage results, but the personal growth and satisfaction that come from using ones skills to serve neighbors and society. At the same time, it seems to me that some aspects of our culture – perhaps related to Calvinism – encourage people to become workaholics, who don't realize they can live well with less; and that they should enjoy the benefits of having time for their own development apart from gainful employment. In my view, self-development is useful work too.

Quality of life issues

Discussing the public good or public purpose is always controversial. This is especially true in a large society that includes every kind of religious and ethical viewpoint, and whose citizens represent widely disparate conditions of education, wealth and experience. A thoughtful series of scholarly lectures/ discussions on this topic – "Modern Money and Public Purpose" – has been going on for two years, under the auspices of Columbia University Law School. The lectures are open to the public, and available in free video recordings on the internet from Modern Money Network.[152] I don't expect that the law will represent everyone's interests equally, of course. The idealistic principle of being 'all inclusive' and a 'melting pot' is easier to talk about (and wave the flag over) than to practice. To complicate it further, such terms don't really have clear meaning, even in the abstract. Conceptions of an ideal society change as science and technology bring once utopian dreams (or dystopian nightmares) into the realm of possibilities. However, I'll conclude this section with a few more themes of 'public goods' that can loosely be called 'quality of life' issues. These 'progressive' ideas will doubtless raise objections by many readers, but they are worth some thought.

Healthy environment

Few people would suggest that air quality is a local issue, although local air conditions certainly vary. Nor can people reasonably claim that volcanos in Iceland, forest fires in Arizona, coal emissions in China, deforestation in Brazil or mono-crop agriculture, chemical pesticides and 'genetically modified organisms' (GMOs) in agriculture processes in the U.S. and elsewhere don't affect people in places distant from where they originate. Yet despite these obvious facts, there are people who deny these and other environmental problems, or else claim that the federal government should stay uninvolved.

To make any reasonable judgment about proposals of environmental regulation demands two things that are hard to find. The first is reliable information. The second is sound judgment about costs and benefits. To illustrate the problem of information, think of the emotional coverage of environment topics like global warming, Alaskan oil drilling, wind farms, mercury in Great Lakes fish, agricultural pesticides, genetically modified organisms, and "fracking". Are they even truly issues? What ideas are disseminated by the media about such questions, and how can the public judge their validity? I'll just mention one strange case, to illustrate the silliness of much that passes for scientific thinking. A young acquaintance recently brought up an environmental topic about which he was concerned, and encouraged me to check it out. It dealt with "chemical trails" being sprayed from high flying aircraft over large areas of several states – especially near some military air force bases.

These so-called "chemtrails" which are similar to condensation trails ('contrails') but longer lasting, are believed to prove that planes are spraying toxic chemicals into the air, for various undisclosed (and dark) purposes of the government and military. The idea is nonsense, I'm sure, but numberless people believe it. It is a 'conspiracy theory', that began about 1996 and has been gaining popularity. Just a few weeks ago (on July 1, 2013) another flurry of media reports stated that Edward Snowden – the American fugitive in Russia, wanted for releasing government secrets to *WikiLeaks* – had confirmed the United States government involvement in chemtrail programs. Such conspiracy thinking is not limited to America; reports about chemtrails come from around the world, and are attributed to other governments as well.

In one sense, it seems impossible to research chemtrails objectively. There is too much data. My first Google search brought about five million entries! Of the few dozen I examined, almost all of them bemoan the fact of chemtrails, and try to explain why and by whom they are being used. I'm grateful for *Wikipedia*, which is among the first few websites to appear in the search, which effectively discredited all the believers. Should I trust *Wikipedia* against the rest? Yes, because it uses transparent, reputable sources, and good reasoning to explain and debunk the hoax, and it is continually edited and corrected. For ordinary information, *Wikipedia* is wonderfully helpful. If one needs more serious research, the references will point the way. *Wikipedia* says:

> Supporters of this conspiracy theory speculate that the purpose of the chemical release may be for solar radiation management, psychological manipulation, population control, weather control or biological warfare/ chemical warfare and that these trails are causing respiratory illnesses and other health problems.[153]

On the believer side, Global Skywatch[154] is one of thousands of websites dedicated to advancing (and profiting from) this myth. In includes a full length "documentary" on the topic. If one is looking for some entertainment, this is a fun place to start; but I recommend it as a good example of what charlatans are all about, how gullible and ignorant many people can be, and how important education is to our national wellbeing.

Healthy bodies, lifestyles and attitudes

Health care is an enormous issue around the world and in America. In one way or another it gets into every discussion about debt and fiscal policy. As usual, the rhetoric runs from unrealistically idealistic to harsh and selfish. The Constitution of the World Health Organization of the United Nations begins with this statement:

> THE STATES Parties to this Constitution declare, in conformity with the Charter of the United Nations, that the following principles are basic to the happiness, harmonious relations and security of all peoples:
>
> Health is a state of complete physical, mental and social wellbeing and not merely the absence of disease or infirmity.

Just on the surface of it, "complete physical, mental and social well-being" is impossible for any government to guarantee, and unreasonable to advocate. But at the other extreme, thinking that health is totally the responsibility of individual citizens, regardless of their wealth and circumstance, is to ignore one of the fundamentals of any society – i.e., mutual protection and care. In any case, the present state of American health leaves much to be desired. And that says nothing about health care, whether public or private. Without going into any detailed suggestions about how to meet societal health problems, or criticism of particular plans to solve them, let me mention a few relevant factors.

First, Americans on average know little about health or how to maintain it. And this is exacerbated by what some call the "institutionalization" of America (and other developed Western nations). It's the natural tendency of all institutions to advance themselves by discovering (or inventing) problems that require their services to solve.[155] This is especially true of institutionalized medicine, whether public, private or 'alternative'. The *modus operandi* of all marketing starts with this idea: make people think they have a problem, and offer to solve it.

Second, to be fair to the conservative perspective, many people are lazy and resistant to doing the hard work of healthy living. And they are often illiterate about health matters.[156] Many companies have initiated employee wellness programs, and offer incentives to take part in them. Yes, it is to their financial benefit to have healthy workers, but nonetheless these programs are generally helpful. Not surprisingly, some liberal agencies like the American Civil Liberties Union (ACLU) will characterize these efforts as domineering and paternalistic (not-to-mention self-serving).[157] But health and health care are not just matters of convenience or preference. Somehow bad habits and bad information need to be improved. This is not just a private matter.

Third, Americans are led to believe they have the best possible health care as a nation, which simply isn't true.[158] Perhaps this opinion comes from the natural pride, which is common everywhere, to believe one's own country (or religion, or race, or musical preference, or culture) is the best. Be that as it may, there are certainly interest groups that benefit from the belief that ours is the best health care system in the world, and resist efforts to reform it, even while advertising that citizens should demand more and more services and buy better and better medications. Physicians groups, insurance providers, health centers, and all businesses who feel threatened by the prospect of making their workers and clients less dependent on them or their services, will try to control public opinion on these questions. The reasons are easy to see. When corporate and individual taxes are increased to take care of public health, it puts a strain on profits and personal wealth, even though healthy workers are more productive.

Assessing health care is a tricky business. It depends on what indicators and factors are considered. Cultural differences affect health, such as attitudes towards birth control, or life in large cities, or sources of information, or tastes in cuisine, or even what body shape is attractive. Country size and population density count. Whether life is near the sea or in farmland or mountains makes a difference.

Nevertheless, given all these variables, I think it's safe to say, as the Urban Institute report of 2009 concluded, that the United States health care system is not the world's best, nor is it even exceptional in any of the areas examined. Nor is it likely that any serious efforts to reform the system will somehow put its good qualities, e.g. technology advancement, at risk.[159]

Let me give some relevant data. Compared to the thirty member nations of the Organization for Economic Coordination and Development (OECD), the U.S. ranks below average in prevention, screening and childhood vaccination rates. It is also low in longevity. At 79 (average of men and women), it ranks below Great Britain, Germany, France, Portugal, Belgium, Ireland, Australia, Sweden, Israel, Italy, Greece, Japan (of course) and two dozen other nations.[160] Relatedly, it ranks low in child survival (i.e.it is high in child mortality). It also ranks below average in the number of hospital beds, the number of hospital discharges, the number of days spent in hospitals, and the number of doctors per one thousand citizens.[161]

As one might expect, the U.S. ranks high in the number of CT and MRI tests, knee replacements, coronary bypasses, Caesarian sections and other costly high tech procedures. The technical quality of these procedures is good, but not outstanding. But general health of the population in America is below average. Patient safety is not up to average. Care for chronic diseases, like asthma, is below average. Until this year, obesity rates in the US were the highest of the OECD nations; but Mexico took the lead recently.[162]

Finally, in my view, the two most important shortcomings of American health care are the inequality of its availability, and its cost inefficiency. There are only two countries in the OECD group – Turkey and Mexico – which have a higher percentage of uninsured citizens than the U. S. At 20% of the population under age sixty-five, this amounts to forty-five million people. The recently enacted Affordable Care Act has as its primary goal to extend health care to these people, yet it has been constantly attacked by the Republicans who have vowed to repeal the entire law, even as it is being haltingly and clumsily implemented.

Their major complaint is that the country can't afford it. That seems like a weak claim when so many poorer countries do afford it. And as I've tried to show, affordability is not an economic issue in a country with fiat currency powers. Even so, there is validity in saying American healthcare costs are exorbitant.

The cost of American healthcare in 2012 – over $8000 per person annually – is two and a half times the average in the OECD nations. It's more than twice the amount spent per person in Great Britain, Belgium, France, Sweden and Ireland, and almost twice as much as in Germany and Australia. At 18% of GDP, total medical expenses in America are double the OECD average. Our hospital costs are 60% higher than average. And for those who are insured, American's receive only about half of the recommended procedures for their ailments. A major reason for this, I believe, is that in the United States, more than half the health expenditures are in the private sector, whereas in the other developed countries, private sector health expenses average one quarter of the total. Great Britain's private costs are 18% of the total. As I write this, today's *New York Times* front page features 'medical tourism' in the context of the cost discrepancies among countries. A man who needed a hip replacement found a bargain price in Belgium. His total cost for the travel, hospital, surgery and rehab care was $14,000; in the United States it would have been $78,000.[163]

Healthy society: quality of life

Before ending this section on issues of fiscal policy and public purpose, it seems appropriate to step back and look again at what public goal setting involves. Everyone has dreams about a happy life, and folk songs are loaded with images of the 'Big Rock Candy Mountain'. In terms of setting policy, no doubt fiscal conservatives and libertarians are leery, and properly so, about thoughts of

'Wouldn't it be nice if …?' They will answer, 'Yes, it would be nice, but we don't have the money, and besides, too much government assistance controls too many people's lives, and makes them dependent and lazy'.

I don't advocate a viewpoint that is unrealistically idealistic, or that concentrates on unachievable goals. I understand the disdain skeptical critics express for social advocacy organizations which they characterize as "feel good" groups who sit around the campfire singing Kumbaya[164] But critics need to remember that all the normal monetary measurements of success ultimately rest on notions of social and environmental conditions that will be 'good to have'. So a new area of research has evolved into just what factors can measure those conditions effectively. We'll look briefly at some of this development, to keep in mind when discussing appropriate fiscal policy.

Marc Miringoff was influential in American social science efforts to assess and evaluate a society's changes in measurable terms, which could provide international perspective and cross-national comparisons – an area that is often called 'quality of life' (QOL) research. He and colleagues at Fordham University developed an "Index of Social Health", which went through several publications, starting in 1987, with the last one in 2010. Miringoff died in 2004. In a *New York Times* obituary, Eduardo Porto summarized Miringoff's contributions and concerns:

> In a lecture in 2001, he noted that if progress were to be measured only in terms of gross domestic product, the performance of the stock markets and other narrow economic measures, we would be "missing most of what makes life miserable, interesting or good." His new indicator painted a novel picture of the nation's prosperity, confirming that economic growth and social progress did not always go hand in hand.

Dr. Miringoff's social index plummeted to a low of 38 out of 100 in 1993, from a high of 77 out of 100 in 1973, notwithstanding 20 years of per capita income growth. Since then, the nation has recorded progress, according to Dr. Miringoff's index, which jumped back to 54 in 2000 only to drop back to 46 in 2001. "It used to be that a rising tide lifted all boats, but at a certain point during the 70's, social health and per-capita income split apart," Dr. Miringoff said in an interview with The New York Times in 2000. "And this may be the result of the new economy: the loss of steady, well-paid jobs with benefits for less-skilled blue collar workers."

Since the 1980's, other groups have developed alternative indexes of social health using different sets of variables. Dr. Miringoff's social health index was adopted by state officials in Connecticut to measure social problems and formulate policies. [165]

Statistics are boring to read, hard to interpret, and easy to abuse. But in this era of increasingly strident emotional political bickering, full of anger and prophesies of doom all sides, statistics may offer a measure of objectivity in discussing fiscal policies and societal wellbeing. With that in mind, I'll simply close this chapter with some text and graphics from the latest "Index of Social Health" of the Institute for Innovation in Social Policy (IISP) which is now at Vassar College, for the reader to consider. [166]

The Index of Social Health

The Index of Social Health, the centerpiece of the Institute's work, monitors the social well-being of American society. It has been released annually by the Institute (formerly the Fordham Institute for Innovation in Social Policy) since 1987. Like the Index of Leading Economic Indicators or the Gross Domestic

Product, it is a composite measure that combines multiple indicators to produce a single number for each year.

The Index of Social Health is based on sixteen social indicators. These are: infant mortality, child abuse, child poverty, teenage suicide, teenage drug abuse, high school dropouts, unemployment, weekly wages, health insurance coverage, poverty among the elderly, out-of-pocket health costs among the elderly, homicides, alcohol-related traffic fatalities, food insecurity, affordable housing, and income inequality.

The premise of the Index is that American life is revealed not by any single social issue, but by the combined effect of many issues, acting on each other. In looking at social problems that affect Americans at each stage of life childhood, youth, adulthood, and the elderly—as well as problems that affect all ages, the Index seeks to provide a comprehensive view of the social health of the nation.

Most Recent Findings

In 2010 (the last year for which complete data are available), the Index of Social Health stood at 48.8 out of a possible 100—down 2.2 points from the previous year and 9.5 points from the most recent peak in 2007. This score is the lowest in fourteen years. Overall, between 1970 and 2010, the Index declined from 64.7 to 48.8, a drop of 24.5 percent.

The recent decline of the Index reflects, among other things, the impact of the economic recession that hit the country in late 2007. Although the recession officially ended in 2009, social indicators often take longer to recover, so we expect to see further declines in the Index when complete statistics for 2011 become available.

The followinng tables and graph show, from 1970 to 2011, social conditions have on average held even or declined slightly, and the Institution for Innovation in Social Policy predicts they will decline further when the new data is examined. This supports my non-scientific view of American society at present. The next chapter will examine what I believe to be the most important, effective and practical arena in which to deal with the social problems this study has discussed – i.e., education.

Progress and Lack of Progress

Seven indicators have improved since 1970:	Nine indicators have worsened since 1970:
Infant mortality	Child poverty
High school dropouts	Child abuse
Teenage drug abuse	Teenage suicide
Poverty, ages 65 and over	Unemployment
Homicides	Weekly Wages
Alcohol-related traffic fatalities	Health insurance coverage Out-of-pocket health costs,
Affordable housing	ages 65 and over Food insecurity
	Income inequality

The following graph shows the changes in the Index of Social Health in the period – roughly the past 40 years – with which this study has been most interested.

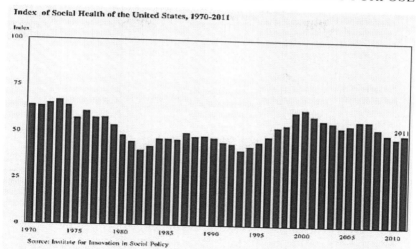

Index of Social Health of the United States, 1970-2011

Source: Institute for Innovation in Social Policy

Chapter Nine

Education and a Good Society

Education is the answer

Education is the answer; but what what questions does it answer? This chapter will propose that education is the best way to solve issues we've been examining which are traceable to unjust and socially harmful consequences of "financializing everything", and its related upward redistribution of wealth. But education is more than a practical tool to helping ordinary citizens meet the increasing costs of daily life – i.e., a way to a better better job and income. It's also a public, and a personal good. It's a public good, as a means to a better society. Indeed, education is fundamentally necessary for a true democracy to be possible, rather than a misunderstood myth to appease passive citizens and give them a false sense of influencing government. And education is personal good, insofar as without it, no individual can be genuinely free, or fulfill her potential to control her own choices and actions. That requires both self-knowledge, and seeing objectively what is valuable. As Socrates said long ago, "An unexamined life is not worth living."

I hasten to emphasize that education is not equivalent to schooling, although they are often linked. Paradoxically, education is both too important to leave out of national fiscal policy discussions, and too important to leave in the hands of government bureaucracies. My prejudice in favor of education must have been evident from the start of this essay. I believe that if enough people were sufficiently educated, with the right coordination, they would be able to solve every issue we've analyzed here. This proves both my bias and my idealism. I'll try to support this claim and this prejudice, by showing what I think education entails – especially education for society – together with some of the problems that get in the way.

Reality, truth and knowledge

To ground this critique of education, a little abstract metaphysics, psychology and epistemology are appropriate. But first, some basic terms need defining: "reality," "truth," and "knowledge." Reality is 'the way things are', or all that is the case, or the cosmos – i.e., this world, and any other worlds or realms that may exist, including the mental and/ or the spiritual. Reality comes to our consciousness in various ways, and wakens our minds to have what we call the experience of sensations, memories, emotions, fantasies, images, concepts and many other 'mental' ideas. I personally think that 'experience', properly so called, cannot exist apart from language. At least, I've not met or heard of any person who could recall any experience that occurred before she or he knew language; but that is a difficult thing to analyze and test.

With language, people join words together, and do things with the result. They ask questions, express feelings, make demands, and of course, make statements. Statements may or may not express the way a person experiences the world, or in other words, what she thinks reality is. Nor do statements necessarily mirror reality. They may be deceitful, or they may be mistaken. In either case, if a statement does in fact mirror the world ('the way things are' or 'reality'), it is a *true* statements. If not, it is *false*. But true statements are not the reality they mirror. They represent it, mentally.

Truth then is not a thing. It's a characteristic or quality of statements, or better, of 'beliefs' 'claims' or 'opinions' about reality that are contained in those statements. 'The truth about X' is our store of (true) beliefs about X. This is one kind of knowledge. Some people have more of it; others less. They are more or less 'knowledgeable' or 'learned.' We could say that true statements mirror the form of reality. In any case, our *knowledge* is our collection of *true beliefs* about *reality*; it is our connection with reality. And it is *mental*, only. The knowledge I've described here is just one kind of knowledge - conceptual knowledge, which is very useful. Science is conceptual knowledge. But it too is indirect. It may present a 'true opinion' of reality, but that is not reality; it is a mental *representation* of reality. Is it even possible to get *direct* knowledge of reality? It depends on what kind of reality one is searching for. In the case of 'ultimate reality', mystics like to say it can be experienced, but that's a subject for a different discussion. It is a topic that belongs to "epistemology" – the philosophy of knowing. Education is allegedly about knowing, and since the topic here is the role of education in a good society, some epistemology seems necessary. Let me illustrate a little.

Plato distinguished among beliefs (or 'mere opinions'), true beliefs, and knowledge.[167] Suppose I believe that the shortest route from Chicago to New York is to go east; my belief happens to be true. For practical purposes, true belief works as well as knowledge. If I want to travel between these cities, or tell someone else how to do so, true belief will get the right result. But my belief could be false as easily as true; it's a matter of luck. I contend that belief, whether or not it happens to be correct belief, can't be knowledge, because knowledge is not a matter of luck. Knowledge requires that I have good reasons for my belief, and that I 'know that I know'. This is why I don't find most of education to be beneficial, and why it is so hard to get students to learn. Memorizing facts, even if they are true, is not what develops a mind, or helps a person to be a creative and useful member of society.

Kinds of knowing/ levels of thinking

I've been speaking about knowledge in abstract terms, I realize. People use the term "know" casually in different ways, and each has its place in every life. I can 'know' – i.e. be acquainted with – my cousin Mae in Louisiana, or I can 'know' Central Park in New York. I can 'know' – i.e. be skilled in – tango, or bridge. I can 'know' – i.e. memorize – a song lyric, or the state capitals. And I can know – i.e. understand – history, calculus, psychopharmacology or astrophysics.

The knowledge that is needed to understand problems in our economic system, to judge where the public good lies, and to devise means to improve things requires high levels of cognition, reasoning, critical analysis, creativity, judgment and experience. Obviously no one excels in all kinds of learning. Collaborative learning is basic to the success of private and public institutions, and is demanded of every level of government which tries to build useful programs and make rules to help society.

Certainly not everyone needs to be a philosopher; but please remember that a philosophical mindset – i.e. rational, objective and undogmatic approach to finding truth – is what started the core of western democratic society, as well as the development of science. It can help to direct current society back onto a course that is better than the one it is apparently now taking. I'm not talking about some 'back to basics' movement, which will take care of itself, but a 'back to thinking well' movement, which won't just happen.

Most people believe things because they have been told to, or because they want to believe. It makes their lives smoother if they agree with, and follow their parents', or teachers,' or priests,' or governors' claims, until they get old enough to do what they want instead of what they were told to do. But these attitudes hamper knowledge and frustrate personal growth, and the public good. Without good thinking skill. and the discipline it requires, adults abandon their 'schooling' as irrelevant (and it often is so), and turn to gratifying themselves without real knowledge of consequences. The culture that results is characterized by aimlessness, selfishness, irresponsibility, trivial pursuits, and irrational competition for recognition In the unemployed and segregated inner cities and the backwater communities of rustbelt towns, aimlessness and competition add brutal violence to the already unhappy mix. I believe that if schools left students with nothing more than how to think well – i.e. how to analyze, find reasons for, and judge objectively what they experience and are told (or read) – these ailments would start to heal by themselves. However, objectivity is increasingly rare.

In recent academic social science, it has become fashionable to say that objectivity is an artificial attitude, and in fact truth is always *subjective*, not *objective*. This, of course, filters down into the way college students think, and it's attractive because it supports their belief in their own feelings. I strongly disagree with this view (which is itself only an opinion), but it permeates much of western culture. It is primarily a sophisticated way of justifying relativism – i.e., the view that every claim about what is good, or moral, or valuable is only a matter of 'perspective'. In its more radical and destructive form it is also the belief that there is no truth, and that every idea is simply a matter of opinion and perspective. I won't get into the arguments here. I will only underscore how much harder this view makes any search for knowledge, in the hopes of improving society.

'Educating for society' is a reachable national goal

'Educating for society' means something different from 'educating society,' or just 'education.' I want to emphasize that education can and should be neither an individual activity, independent of others, nor mass indoctrination, ignoring individuality. I think it requires a philosophy that concentrates on individual development, while acknowledging that a person is not whole unless she sees herself as having a place in, and a responsibility to society; and that she can't learn without the perspective of other people's views. Education is a collaborative project, with outcomes that change both individuals and their communities. And apart from questions of schooling, education can be a lifelong, useful and pleasant habit. Perhaps these thoughts sound like the dreams of a utopian. I think they are achievable goals, which have been suggested in one form or another by many people for the past couple of centuries, and have succeeded here and there, on a small scale, when communities and individuals were willing to experiment. I personally have read about, seen and experienced some educational efforts that were wonderful, some that were mediocre, and some that were poor.

Some paradoxes of educating for society

Educating for society depends on political will, practical means, and especially knowledge of the problems which are harming the nation at present. Paradoxically, these all depend on education. This looks circular, and it is. Let's look at a few relevant paradoxes.

A deluded citizenry doesn't know it's deluded

In principle, citizens of a democracy have the last word to determine what laws they wish to live by, and to improve conditions that are problematic. However, this can happen only if they understand the problems correctly. A corrupt system tries to maintain secrecy, and works to keep citizens ignorant. This is true of all societies, but especially so in democracies, because corrupt persons cannot operate with impunity without fear of public censure, despite their positions of power. The first paradoxical problem, then, is this: citizens must reform the system in order to get the knowledge they need to reform it.

It's difficult, but not impossible, for a person to get good information despite the barrage of disinformation and mistaken ideas circulating throughout the society, especially in the popular media, which seem to be the first sources ordinary people turn to when they take an interest in learning. How can a person decide which ideas are true, among the myriads that are immediately available? In my view, true ideas are those which can be 'verified', but what constitutes verification is a matter of dispute.

A wise person 'knows she doesn't know'

Having what might be called a traditional perspective, I think truth exists, even though our efforts to find it are halting and full of errors. How will I 'recognize' some truth or other as being true, unless I know in advance what it is I'm looking for? This sounds like another paradox – and in fact it was famously mentioned by Plato (with tongue in cheek) in the *Meno*.[168] But there is another closely related problem about knowledge, also found in the *Meno*, about which Plato was completely serious. Genuine knowledge can only come to a person who is modest enough to recognize her ignorance and who therefore will continue devotedly searching until she finds good answers.[169] This thought is underscored in the *Apology*, where Socrates, who is about to be condemned to death, describes himself as a philosopher ("wisdom lover"). He recounts at his trial how one of his acquaintances reported that the oracle of Apollo at Delphi told him "no one is wiser than Socrates". He famously and modestly explains to the jury what he thinks the oracle's statement meant:

> [B]ut the truth really is, gentlemen, that the god in fact is wise, and in this oracle he means that human wisdom is worth little or

nothing, and it appears that he does not say this of Socrates, but simply adds my name to take me as an example as if he were to say that this one of you human beings is wisest, who like Socrates knows that he is in truth worth nothing as regards wisdom.[170]

In every case, only ignorant people can learn; that's logical. But among those, only the people who *admit* their ignorance will *seek* to learn. Those who think they already know will have no reason or motive to learn, and so they will remain ignorant.

The love of learning isn't natural

It's often claimed that children are curious. I disagree, if by curiosity is meant a desire to *know*, or any concern for the *truth*. Children are motivated by the desire for *pleasure*. In the search for pleasure, they stick their noses into everything, and in the process, they learn from experience what brings reward and what doesn't. Their search is not for knowledge as such, but for the *means* – any means, including knowledge – to find pleasure. If they believe it will benefit them, they will accept any story (true or false), and tell any story (true or false), to get their way. If they're well trained by caring adults, they will learn to put off immediate gratification in favor of longer-term rewards. In the long term they may even learn to subordinate self-interest to higher values. This is a life-long process, and apparently many people never complete it.

Knowledge can' be taught; it must be learned

So many conversations I hear, and policy decisions I learn about, involve 'teaching a lesson' to someone, whether it is a recalcitrant regime in Iran or North Korea, or Islamist terrorists in Mali, or a gang in Chicago's Westside communities. The lesson that needs teaching is presumably the idea that 'bad behavior will bring bad consequences'. Sadly, advocates of this lesson – for example politicians, police officers and ARA gun owners – think violence will cure violence. It won't, and it certainly won't teach that violence is a bad first choice.

More generally, force won't teach anyone to believe what a would-be teacher claims. It won't even prove that the teacher believes what she or he is trying to teach. Least of all will it cause the pupil to know whether the teacher's claims are true. As I said above, there are levels of what is called 'knowing'. I do think children can be trained to act and speak certain ways that masquerade as knowledge. Given enough 'reinforcement' (positive or negative), they can be induced to memorize and repeat words by rote. Manifestly this is not knowledge of any serious sort, even though it may involve some learning about the experience itself. And whatever the learner discovers from reflection on the experience is self-taught. Motivation is necessary for learning, but it isn't sufficient. Knowledge demands understanding and confirmation of what is learned. High levels of knowledge include creative analysis, disciplined reasoning and good judgment. Everyone needs help to get there, but the helpers can't do the work of learning.[171]

Learning doesn't come from schools, so what do they do?

The last paradoxical problem for education and social improvement is the idea that *schools do not – indeed cannot – educate people*. I would say that good *teachers* educate people, but even this is misleading. One cannot force another to learn. Good teachers are those who can inspire and motivate students to learn – but the learning is ultimately up to the student. This rule holds increasingly true, as the level of thinking and learning increases; from rote memory and repetition of actions and words (at the start), to analysis and understanding of causes and effects (in the middle), to critical judgment of meaning and value (at the top). All this follows from what we have argued above. So what then is the purpose of schools?

The idea of schooling covers a lot of ground and history. We generally think of school as a place for learning, but what is learned, and who controls it depend on the time and cultural context. The word "school" comes from a Greek term *schole* which means "leisure", which has its roots in *schein* ("to have," "to hold"). In other words, school is what you do when your time is your own. In ancient Greece, this meant time for study, self-knowledge and especially self-improvement – not time for doing nothing, or trivial self-indulgence. Aristotle even claimed self-development is life's goal; any occupation is to support that goal, and contribute to society's needs. Relatedly, the classic Greek word for "labor" is *ascholia* ("not-leisure"). The ancient schools of the philosophers, then, were not places for rote learning, job training, or forced conformity to ruling norms. They were places of self-fulfillment, through respectful interaction, reasoning, and striving for the highest level of understanding and wisdom possible. [172]

This idealistic notion of schooling certainly has not been the norm in America, ever, although there have been idealistic leaders and individual institutions. [173] The better schools have always been in communities of wealthy and influential families, and even among these the educational philosophy of self-development mentioned above are seldom found; never in a public school. In Puritan New England, schools were established early, for boys and girls, where basic reading, writing and math were drilled into students' memories, with primers and discipline. Their purpose was to learn religious ideas from Biblical scriptures, and to develop business success.

After 1647, Puritan Massachusetts required every town of fifty homes to provide a 'petty' (elementary) school, and towns of a hundred families needed to add a higher (or grammar) school, where Latin was the college preparation curriculum, up to age fourteen or fifteen. Boston Latin School was the first such 'grammar' school in America – founded in 1635 – and is still running with great prestige and success. Harvard was founded in 1636. In the Middle Atlantic colonies there were private and religious schools to do the same sort of thing, and apprenticeships to take the poorer boys. In the rural

Southern colonies, children of the wealthy were typically home tutored, while poor boys would learn trades as apprentices. Slaves were kept by law from any education.

Private colleges were established for religious teachers and other professional training, including law in some places. The curriculum was "classical" – built around ancient languages and history, mathematics and some science. Most of the graduates were expected to be ministers, or teachers.[174] Women's education lagged behind men's, but by the early 19th century, "republican motherhood" was catching on; families and states could be brought together by educating women to bring national values into their homes and communities. Secular public schools developed later than private schools, and their goals have generally been different from private schools. Free elementary schools were in all the states by the time of the Civil War, although their management and funding was up to local towns. In rural areas, where most people lived, these were often one room "common schools" without distinction of age or gender.

Between the 1890's and the start of World War I lies the so-called "Progressive Era". which expressed a secular, more inclusive, gender neutral and practical philosophy of education, differing widely from the classical approach.[175] It was a period of enormous growth of cities, industrialization and immigration (all related closely). To meet these demographic changes, public high schools multiplied. Public educators' role was to acculturate the new citizens, provide general knowledge for flexibility of employment and management needs, and to offer specific 'vocational skills' for those who would not go on to more schooling.

Many land grant colleges and public universities were developed in the late 19th century, primarily to support the very practical work of agriculture, engineering and teacher training. And around the turn of the 20th century, prestigious private universities were founded outside of New England, like Stanford, Johns Hopkins, Carnegie Mellon, University of Chicago, Vanderbilt and Duke – generally endowed by philanthropic business leaders. All of these were secular, scientific and technological institutions, oriented to develop the kinds of research, technology and business applications which could build the economy. This has been the nature of American public schools and higher education for the past century.

Education reform and critical pedagogy

We can see that what schools do depends on what their managers want. 'School reform' is simply a name for efforts to change schools to meet the thinking of the reformers. Reformers have been around a long time. Jan Amos Komensky (Comenius in Latin) is a fine example, but he remains almost unknown in America. (Rembrandt painted his portrait.) He was born in 1592 in Moravia (current Czech Republic), but was forced to move frequently because of shifting political and religious borders during the Thirty Years War. A follower of Hus, he was a leader of the Moravian Brothers. Hoping to make Protestant education as effective as Jesuit education was for Catholics, he established schools, taught, lectured, wrote texts (including the first picture books), and advised governmental agencies in his travels. He was also a political scientist, a feminist, a pacifist, and although he came out of poverty, he gave liberally to good causes out of his own means. [176]

Like the later Enlightenment thinkers, Komensky believed that humans can be improved, and that the "light" of learning can eliminate conditions of war, about which he was so aware. In this he was out of the mainstream of Calvinist Protestant thinking. He became associated with the Pansophic or Encyclopedic Movement, which undertook to organize all knowledge, with the view to being able to discover the laws hidden within the collected data. When he visited England, to take part in a parliamentary commission on education reform in 1641, he met John Winthrop the Younger, from Boston, who invited him to be president of Harvard University, which had been founded a few years previous. But Komensky didn't accept.[177] Around 1660 he wrote something I've been trying to show throughout this discussion:

> If men were shown what their complete and real good is, they would be drawn to it. Were they, moreover, shown the right means for its achievement, an all-inclusive and all-satisfying philosophy, religion and statecraft would be fully attained.[178]

Jacques Barzun comments that Komensky was doing what school reformers always do in one way or another. Schools "ossify" over time, and must periodically be jolted back to life. In his book, *From Dawn to Decadence*, Barzun states:

> The reason for the loss of vitality is that the school is a government on a small scale; it aims at forming a common mind as government aims at a common will. Both need periodic overhaul, a re-injection of the original idea that got lost in routine.[179]

What Barzun doesn't mention here is that educational reform often involves more than a "re-injection of the original idea". It also involves questioning what that original idea was, or what it should be. Are the guiding principles good? Some progressive educators have even suggested that institutions are too frozen in bureaucracy to be reformed. Two of the more radical voices of a generation ago – Ivan Illich in Austria, and Paulo Freire in Brazil – were friends, and Roman Catholic advocates of "liberation theology". Freire's *Pedagogy of the Oppressed* (1968), argues that contemporary educational philosophy is perversely wrong. He worked among illiterate adults, and developed successful programs centering on local cultural groups for teaching peasant farmers to read and write in only a few months, leading his government to start a program of similar cultural circles. Freire says that underclass students are passive and expect to be told what they must know. They are fearful of freedom which they have never known, and need encouragement to take responsibility. The perceived authority of teachers reinforces the passivity of the learners; it makes understanding almost impossible. Students and teachers need to be engaged in an interactive and respect-building relationship. Learning needs to be in an environment that speaks to the students' lived social situation.

Illich's *Deschooling Society* (1971) went so far as to argue that schools must be eliminated from the learning process, and some new mechanisms of learning developed in their place. In fact, his general social criticism rests in the theme that 'institutionalization' has made life sterile, and people passive. Institutions will always interpret life in ways that prove society needs them. This rests on the belief which 'modern' humans have accepted that no problem exists which rational science can't solve. The ancient (primitive) feeling of *hope* has been replaced by the modern feeling of *expectation*. In the business world, the result is equivalent to saying, 'Let's create a need so that we can market a product to meet that need'. The same applies to the medical world, the social work world, and the world of public assistance to the needy. Of course, the needy are trained to expect this aid, and are put into a passive mode of life and thought by the process. And they make political demands accordingly.

Surreptitiously, reliance on institutional process has replaced dependence on personal good will. The world has lost its humane dimension and reacquired the factual necessity and fatefulness which were characteristic of primitive times. But while the chaos of the barbarian was constantly ordered in the name of mysterious, anthropomorphic gods, today only man's planning can be given as a reason for the world being as it is. Man has become the plaything of scientists, engineers, and planners.[180]

Freire, Illich and other reformers have introduced "critical pedagogy" into educational philosophy. Its main point is that universal education – long a stated goal of every developed nation – is impossible so long as the educational system imposes the views of the dominant class and culture. Indeed, Illich is against 'universal education', if by that is meant compulsory schooling for everyone; although he favors 'universal opportunity for education'. Poor people will never be able to share fairly in, or contribute to, the public good so long as they are kept in school environments that try – and fail – to indoctrinate them into conformity with middle-class values and beliefs, as expressed in typical curricular structure, texts, writing assignments, activities, tests, not to mention how to behave in class, be respectful, turn in assignments and so forth. These 'rules' contradict and demean the everyday experiences, survival skills and attitudes of the underclass students, and even make them incapable of understanding or responding favorably. It's a disservice to the whole society as presently practiced.

The only hope, it is said, is to "empower" students to understand and be critical of their situation enough to be able to contribute to its improvement and their own. This 'critical thinking' shared by students and teachers, is real life social criticism. It is not the sterilized 'white bread' version of critical thinking that is regular school fare – i.e. logic and reasoning designed to enable students to solve mathematical and scientific problems, and become good producers and consumers. [181]

Schools should not be businesses

As I said elsewhere, these problems of education and educational reform are not new. But I believe that in the last three or four decades they have intensified, concurrent with economic issues we have already noted, such as unchecked growth in the financial sector, increasing inequity of wealth distribution, and unfair power in the hands of oligarchs. There is little doubt that schools are viewed more and more through the mind set of business administration, by their executives, their communities and their taxpayer supporters. Business jargon comes glaringly into all the conversations and policies about schools, in the efforts to make them efficient and profitable, especially in the public sector. It is present in the vision of the 'product' schools turn out (i.e. graduates who are attractive employees and eager consumers); in the 'productivity' of the employees (i.e. teachers and staff); and in the 'satisfaction of their customers' (i.e. students and parents who pay tuition). These values are good in their place. And of course, finding useful and gainful employment is necessary and beneficial to both workers and the society. But I don't think a good society, or even a successful and wealthy society, will be the end result of the erosion of educational values other than money.

Recent political campaigns and legislation in Indiana and Wisconsin demeaned the merits of union organization among public employees, and specifically teachers. There has been a campaign from the conservative side that implies teachers should be agents who, like obedient factory workers, carry out the business plan (or the curriculum) of their school. This goes back to the idea that education can be imposed on students, and that they can be made to buy into the ideas that the governing boards of directors and local school boards have chosen. This is mistaken on both counts. First, the curriculum needs to fit the needs of the students, and the communities in which they operate. They should not have to conform to standards of success that are artificial, and one-sidedly money oriented. And secondly, students can't be forced to learn; but they can be motivated to try to learn, if their teachers are effective and concerned models for them. Teaching that results in learning is the result of personal relationships – not mechanical processes imposed by a curriculum.

Teaching is hard to do well, and not surprisingly, good teachers burn out, especially when they are under the pressures of fiscal demands, in poor communities, where students think they are bound to fail, and teachers feel responsible for the fact. It is not improved when rules for success are imposed by bureaucracies, and governed by politicians whose policies represent special interests and not the public good. I read recently a book by Peter McLaren – *Life in Schools.* [182] It's a diary and critique of his introduction to teaching in one of the lowest income immigrant neighborhoods of Toronto. In one place, he reported what his supervisor and close friend had told him after a meeting with the principle. The school board was working on a curriculum that would be "teacher proof". That's one of the saddest outcomes I can imagine for contemporary public education.

How much education is enough?

This lengthy critique of American education was written to support my belief that our society cannot improve itself until it sees its problems clearly, and discovers the best means for correcting them. That requires education of the citizenry, of course, but education is difficult both at the individual level and certainly so in the aggregate. I don't know of any meaningful estimates of the size of the population that needs to be well educated, nor what their level of education is necessary to see the problems clearly, and to consider their solutions objectively. Is there some sort of critical mass or tipping point of good thinking that will translate into good public policy? I don't know.

After a long, long teaching career I remain stubbornly sure of a few things about good education:

(1) it's not just another product to sell in our consumerist culture;

(2) it's not primarily to help us get what we want, but to know what we should want;

(3) it is not about private beliefs, personal goals or competition; it is about objectivity, tolerance and modesty;

(4) we can't find freedom, fulfillment or happiness without knowing reality, and education is ultimately the search for reality;

(5) what children and most adults think is real isn't;

(6) finding reality is not natural or easy;

(7) no one can become educated who doesn't want to be;

(8) teachers cannot educate, but they can point the way, and inspire.

Speaking in terms of any person's growth, welfare and happiness, I'm sure there is no limit to the value of learning throughout life. And many fine academics have researched and experimented in the past, and continue to research and experiment about the nature of learning, and propose philosophies and methodologies of education.[183] Speaking in practical terms, ordinary citizens can certainly get along without being academically sophisticated about worldly matters, or understanding high levels of abstract philosophy.

The problem for this study, however, is to critique the nature, extent and effects of inequality and indebtedness in our society, in regard both to economy and morality, and to clarify the degenerating state of affairs in both regards. It's my contention that few people know what is going on, in and out of public view, which aids and abets this degeneration. It is with that belief in mind that I have always pushed the practical importance – in fact necessity – of working to educate "the public" enough to have them demand improvement.

To be realistic, it's easier to stir emotions in order to move people to action than it is to convince them rationally that action is needed. Many people are practiced at the former. But in my opinion, fomenting revolution through appeal to emotion is usually a bad idea. People suffer greatly in revolutionary violence. Leaders of violent revolutions are often cruel, and intolerant of opposition. And they frequently hold onto power after the revolution has taken place. None of this benefits a society. Finally, ours is meant to be a society of open debate, and freely chosen laws, rather than forced conformity. However, if people are pushed far enough, whether or not they understand the causes of their dissatisfaction, violence is a possibility, even in America. Recently an acquaintance drew my attention to a poem by Carl Sandburg: "I am the People, The Mob." I recommend it to the reader. Beware the sleeping giant.

This long essay may be helpful to thoughtful readers, if the claims it makes are correct, to provide a framework and perspective for major issues that trouble American society – e.g. inadequate education, unemployment, unfair distribution of political influence, overemphasis on money, overdependence on institutions, loss of community, and violence. At the national level, these issues are further confused by misconceptions about the availability and allocation of economic and material resources. For me it is an exercise in philosophical thought, but with a practical purpose in mind. I've been trying to discover some general principles to organize my effort to understand and confront these issues, without being overwhelmed by their complexity, or distracted by trivial pursuits which can, I think, make one's life seem meaningless. Our society's individuals, groups and agencies go about solving problems piecemeal, and often for reasons of profit or power. Inevitably, some problems are not interesting to the private economy, in which case the public economy needs to lend a hand.[184] It is the 'bigger' issues that occupy my thinking today, but our lives take place in the real realm of daily interaction – not in philosophical abstractions – and properly so.

There are thousands of 'social critics' who in various ways produce a stream of information, especially by blogs and other contemporary internet media. Perhaps this will turn into a river – even a ground swell or sea change – of public awareness. Scholarly books and journal articles raise the quality of ideas required for a good grasp of trends, their possible causes, and ideas for improvement, but these are not so easily accessible to a wide public. The 'blogosphere' is free, but it's also full of disinformation and emotional venting, so one needs to be careful to check whether ideas are coming from trustworthy sources. In all these 'opinions', including mine, there may be the beginning of a desire for national 'self-examination', for improvement, and for enlightenment on how to bring it about, but it's hard to be optimistic.

One promising development in education is the rapid growth of on-line sources for good learning. Project Gutenberg was perhaps the first of such efforts, founded in 1971 by Michael Hart at the University of Illinois. It provides access to more than 40,000 printed works in the public domain, primarily literature of the western tradition, in English and other languages.[185] Other so-called 'open sources' provide online access to books and academic journals of a wide variety of subject areas. Some of these are free, and others require a modest fee for use. Google Books, and JStorr are examples. TED Talks is another development, started by Richard S. Wurman with a conference in 1984, and annually since 1990, to disseminate "Ideas Worth Spreading". It gives access to video-taped lectures by well-known people on a wide variety of topics.[186]

A further very recent addition involves free on-line courses to the general public. The Khan Academy is one which is geared to high school students, and concentrates on sciences and mathematics. Salman Khan, a Harvard Business School graduate who started this program in 2006, states that it should be a supplement to class room activities and discussion – not a replacement.[187] At the university level, only last year, Harvard and MIT started a collaboration called EdX, soon joined by Stanford and other prestigious schools. A private venture capital enterprise named Coursera announced another consortium including University of Pennsylvania and the University of Michigan, to develop online courses.[188] And only last month, a similar consortium in the U.K. – FutureLearn – was established, which includes some twenty universities.[189] So far, none of these advanced courses is offered for credit, although that is being discussed.

Ultimately, the wellbeing of any country depends on the widest possible dissemination of truth, and the willingness to 'speak truth to power' wherever power is abused. In Chapter 4 above, I underscored

Swedenborg's conviction that a powerful symbolic link exists between *truth* which empowers our moral and spiritual relations and *money* which empowers our material relations. Both can be perverted. Knowledge of that truth is required for both kinds of empowerment, and for the right perspective about their relative value, and ultimately for a sense of indebtedness for whatever portion of both we've received from others (which I would call *wisdom*).

Chapter Ten

For Legislators and Thoughtful Voters

Economics and ethics

I'm not an economist; I'm a philosopher (if that doesn't sound too presumptuous). Having the perspective of a critical thinker – i.e. one trying to get the biggest possible picture of every issue – I approach economics primarily in terms of ethics, and the "public good". Most of us are busily engaged in pursuing our private interests, of which money matters often seem the most concerning and time consuming, but the relationship of 'the economy' to the overall idea of a good society is seldom discussed. Economics (in its more technical forms) is typically taught as part of a business curriculum, or, at the beginning level, as a social science. However, economics has traditionally been part of ethics in the long history of philosophy. Ethics has been my focus in this essay, although at times I've needed to deal with some economic facts and theory – especially macroeconomic theory – that are relevant to the purpose here. I may have tried the reader's patience occasionally when it seemed important to wax technical about debt, and especially about the nature and role of money. Given the current emotional political disputes, especially in America and Europe, these topics are hard to examine with a cool head.

It's understandable that we see frustration and anger, considering the life changing decisions that nations and states are making around the developed world, relating to unemployment, taxes, social programs, and so-called austerity – especially when cultures are clashing violently. I have tried to avoid being too quick to express value judgments that some readers may take ill, which would spoil whatever usefulness this essay might have. I do have opinions about what a good society is, and how to bring it about – opinions that have changed over time. But instead of trying to label my views according to where they lie on the left-to-right spectrum (whatever that means), I prefer to argue for the answers that seem most correct to me, and invite reaction and dialog from anyone interested.

About two hundred years ago, Scottish critic Thomas Carlyle called economics the "dismal science".[190] He was probably reacting to a famous and bleak thesis of his older English contemporary Thomas Malthus – an economist – that world population will inevitably outstrip food sources, resulting in widespread starvation.[191] This thesis, first published in 1798, is questionable, although people continue to be influenced by it, and wonder about 'sustainable' economies. However, I think the really 'dismal' part of economics has to do not with food, which is a concrete thing, but rather with money, which is not, as I've tried to show. The word 'dismal', whose Latin root *dies malus* means "evil days," is very suitable to describe ordinary economics. Debt has always been associated with evil days, one way or another. In addition, I've also tried to show that in relatively recent times – especially during the past forty years when financial sectors of western economies have far outpaced the more productive sectors in terms of profit margins and influence – days have become particularly evil. Possibly some corrective movement will take hold; but that remains to be seen.

The title of this essay includes the word "inequity" in relation to debt and wealth. Inequity literally means 'inequality', as equity means 'equality'; but the words have other meanings too, and many overtones. 'Equity' is a term used in lending, for instance. We speak of having equity in a property, which is its value over and above what is owed by the owner. As many people have experienced in the last five years, equity may go to zero, or even be negative for those properties which are "under water".[192]

As a term in law, equity also has connotations of *justice* and *fairness*; and inequity their opposites. That is, law is not only about what can be objectively documented, proven and measured, but from the beginning has touched on questions of moral value as well. That is because law from the beginning has been associated with what is good for society, as well as the 'higher good' for individuals that religion deals with. Today we distinguish between the civil law and the moral or religious law, but originally, laws and lawyers were not so clearly categorized.[193]

Law is a profession

The law is a *profession*, which is a word we would do well to keep in mind. The first professions were law, medicine, and priesthood, all of which developed in medieval Italy, France, Spain and England under the auspices of the Catholic Church, in the great cathedral schools of the 11th century and onward. A professional was originally a person who *professed* a moral and religious duty to his work, to his associates, and especially to his clients, who were ordinary people at risk (for loss of property, freedom, health, or even life and salvation). Lawyers, doctors and priests were duty bound not to take advantage of their clients. For these reasons, professionals were cautious, among other things, about taking money.

The idea of professional duty has certainly changed since then, especially very recently. I can remember being shocked the first time I saw doctors and lawyers advertise their 'wares'. This occurred suddenly, in about 1977, after a series of court cases at the level of state supreme courts; they were arguing the legal question of professional standards, which had long been a matter of ethics. Even today, some states forbid certain kinds of advertising by lawyers – e.g. 'ambulance chasing'. Originally it was a matter of self-regulation, as part of professional obligation, and not a question of following state laws. For a few old-fashioned professionals, even the increasingly wide-spread use of "codes of ethics" is a denial of the original professional spirit of individual self-discipline and self-regulation. Today, 'professional' simply means anyone who is paid for doing work that requires special skills – even a 'professional wrestler'.

Inequity then has overtones not only of law, but of morality and religious meaning as well. In fact, in Jewish and Christian scriptural language, *inequity* becomes *iniquity,* as I discussed above. In effect this essay has been an effort to understand inequity, and clarify some of the very complex questions about when and why inequity becomes iniquity, and how debt relates to the issue.

Equality and inequality structure our perception

Leaving aside the terms equity and inequity for the moment, with their moral overtones, let's consider the more descriptive concepts of 'equality' and 'inequality', without regard to any problematic social contexts like wealth, education, power, or opportunity (to which we will return). Is it possible to think of equality and inequality, sameness and difference, likeness or unlikeness without implying a preference or a value judgment? "Comparisons are odious" it is said. Equality and inequality seem built into the very way we experience the world, and put ourselves into it, from infancy onward. In fact, human (and animal) thought would be impossible without the primal awareness of sameness and difference. A child orders her world by comparing experiences (sensations), and looking for what is familiar or strange in them – i.e. what is alike or different from, equal or unequal to a previous experience. How does her present sensation compare to previous sensations (which are 'present' in her memory)? Especially, what pleasure or pain might be associated with it?

If a child could not recognize patterns, could she begin to discover the way the world works, and what is connected to what? How else could she begin to *act* so as to re-generate and re-experience the pleasant sensations, and avoid the unpleasant ones? Her mind develops by this process of comparing and ordering sensations (and their memories) according to their sameness or their difference; and in taking purposeful actions that she *expects* will get the same result she experienced previously. Her very earliest efforts will be random, until she finds a pattern. Afterward, her view of the connections may be mistaken; so her expectations may be thwarted by outside forces. Without that awareness, or 'association' of ideas (which may or may not involve 'causation') she would have to lie there and wait passively like a planarian worm for the next sensation, hoping for the best. We couldn't really even call it 'waiting', or 'hoping', since there could be no expectation, hope or worry without awareness of the connections among sensations she remembers. Between one sensation and the next there would be no mental connection, because no ordering by means of memory.[194]

Equality as justice – i.e. as a moral category

Equality enters into our thoughts about justice. In casual conversations, we often hear it said that such-and-such a person is 'not any better than' or is 'no different from' 'the rest of us', and that 'we should all be treated equally, or the same'. But we also hear that 'everyone is different'. These are contradictory claims, of course, and aren't very helpful in a thoughtful discussion. Some kinds of inequality are just. It's not unjust, for example, that men cannot bear children. Some kinds of inequality seem unjust. The question is which kinds? As Aristotle put it, 'Treating unequal people equally is unjust[195]. The difficulty doesn't lie in deciding which equalities or inequalities *exist*, but which ones *matter* – and which kind of inequalities should be eliminated. That involves a specific context. Should gender differences be considered? Well, are you employing firemen ("firepersons"), drafting soldiers, admitting students to college, or hiring servers at Hooters? Should age differences be relevant to those categories? What about differences in education? Or differences in skin color? Or differences in health? Do differences in wealth 'make a difference'? It's doubtful that these questions can be answered once for all time, because the contexts keep changing, along with the relevant (or irrelevant) inequalities.

Value judgments require a standard

Questions like these about equality normally come into considerations of justice. They are value questions – not factual questions – about what is *better* than what, and what is *best*. And so they are notoriously difficult to decide and their discussion in the public sector is always and necessarily conflicted. If they are to be decided at all, as ethical questions, the participants in the conversation must first agree on *standards* of value to guide their reasoning. And they must make it clear, and express, what are those standards (of value, of justice, of 'goodness'). Without such agreement, there can't be any serious rational argument. At best, the conversation will be a waste of time; at worst, it will descend into bickering or even violence.

Without a shared understanding of moral or ethical standards (practically speaking, the terms 'moral' and 'ethical' are synonymous), answering any question will come down to which person (or group) in the dispute has the *power* to force matters in her (or their) favor. That is not the same as finding where the *truth* of the matter lies, or what is the *best* policy. It appears, in our contemporary culture, that the power way is increasingly the normal way of effecting political and social changes – i.e. using force of one sort or another (even if it isn't literally 'taken to the streets'). Perhaps it's the only practical way, but I don't think so. It may sound like an oxymoron but I'm passionate about reason. I hope there better ways to bring some sunlight to our nation's dark and 'evil days'.

In the 'Sixties', I was a naïve and idealistic beginner in education. I often heard fellow teachers say to a class, "I'm not making a value judgment here". For me, this disclaimer seemed to be a strange unwritten rule for people in higher education, who were convinced that true liberality required tolerating every student's values, and accepting her opinion as valid, so to speak, without any judgment. To argue against it was seen as both prejudicial and unsophisticated. So, for example in developing their courses, beginning teachers were careful to be 'value neutral'. They didn't realize that such value neutrality is itself a value; and so are the ideas of not bullying one's classmate, telling the truth, not cheating, and indeed the whole idea of education itself – all of which are ancient and noble values.

My point here is simply that in order to judge which inequalities are unjust and which are not – a primary consideration of law-makers, and those who elect them – it's necessary to have in mind some standard of what justice is. Moreover, since all law-making aims at the "public good", we also need to think about goodness in general – what Plato called The Good – to decide questions of both public good (i.e. justice), and private good (i.e. ethics), which looks at choices and motives of individuals who impact the public good. Leaders and governors at any level of government who propose and discuss public policy, need to be transparent about the values informing their decisions, and not think that somehow such questions are irrelevant to the 'practical nuts and bolts' business of politics and lawmaking.

Such questions are fundamentally relevant, and merit much more rational consideration than is the norm today.

Chicago, March 2014 (updated 2018)

NOTES

[1] See, e.g., Adelaide U. Prof Steven Hail's article in the online journal *The Conversation*, Jan 30, 2017, "Explainer: What is Modern Monetary Theory?"

[2] See, for example, Lambert Strether, "Nothing Natural About the Natural Rate of Unemployment" in *NakedCapitalism*, Nov 26, 2017.

[3] See gunsandbutter.org/transcript-the-slow-crash for a podcast and transcript.

[4] See CNBC online article, "Oxfam says world's richest 1% get 82% of the wealth", Jan 1, 2018.

[5] Michael Hudson, *J is for Junk Economics*, self-published, with Islet-Verlag, 2017.

[6] 1 Preserved in The Datini Archives, Prato, Italy, cited in Stephen Goldblatt, The Swerve (New York: Norton, 2011) p. 114. Ironically, today Prato is a center of the "Slow Food" movement in Italy.

[7] See Adam Davidson and Alex Blumberg, "The Giant Pool of Money," This American Life, Part 355, May 9, 2008 on WBEZ Radio Chicago (and other NPR stations).

[8] R. R. Kelley, "Where Can $700 B in Waste be Cut Annually from the US Healthcare System?" Thompson-Reuters White Paper, October 2009, later expanded to "A Path to Eliminating $3.6 Trillion in Wasteful Healthcare Spending," June 2010, which gives a longer-term analysis.

[9] Christopher Hedges, *Death of the Liberal Class* (NYC: Nation Books, 2010.

[10] See, e.g. Colleen A. Sheehan, "Madison v. Hamilton: The Battle over Republicanism and the Role of Public Opinion" in *The American Political Science Review*, Vol. 98, No 3 (August 2004), pp. 405-424.

[11] Harry Shearer interviewed Stephanie Skelton on *Le Show*, October 28, 2012 (Transcript available on line).

[12] See www.neweconomicperspectives.org.

[13] See my student handout, "Critical Thinking" at Scribd.com (*www.scribd.com/doc/99536140/Critical-Thinking*).

[14] Margaret Atwood, *Payback – Debt and the Shadow Side of Wealth* (Toronto: House of Anansi Press, 2008).

[15] Hernando de Soto, *The Mystery of Capital* (New York: Basic Books, 2003).

[16] Feudalism is a term that covers many cultures, and a long history. For our purposes, this is a simple overview. See T. J. Byrnes and Harbans Mukhia, *Feudalism and Non-European Societies*, Library of Peasant Studies No. 8 (Oxford, U.K.: Psychology Press, 1985).

[17] See *Wikipedia*, "Serfdom".

[18] For a convincing critique of the 'neoclassical' view, see David Graeber, "On the Invention of Money - Notes on Sex, Adventure, Monomaniacal Sociopathy, and the True Function of Economics," blog posted in *Naked Capitalism*, September 12, 2011.

[19] See the blogsite *Michael-Hudson.com*, for topics such as Phoenician interest taking, and Phoenician influence on Greek and Roman trade practices. Also see *Wikipedia*, "Spice Trade" for a well-written history of Arab/ India trade in the Red sea and the Indian Ocean; overland routes closed by Muslims in Egypt and Arabia; and Ottoman conquest of Byzantium in 1453, which cut off European (Venetian) control of major land and sea routes.

[20] Cf. *Wikipedia* under "weregild;" *Wikipedia* under "solidus;" and the Capitulary of Aix-la-Chapelle of 797.

[21] Cf. *history.ac.uk/richard/about*, Institute of Historical Research, and Arts and Humanities Research Council, "Edward III and his contribution to Richard II's treasure".

[22] FIRE (Financial, Insurance and Real Estate) industries, are primarily designed to generate profits through ownership, investments and interest-generating activities, rather than making goods or offering services.

[23] Karl Marx criticized the social effects of capitalism in his day very effectively, whatever one thinks of his economics or his socialist goals.

[24] I.e. after the Norman Conquest of England in 1066.

[25] Harold J. Laski, "Early History of the Corporation in England," Harvard Law Review 56 (1917) p. 562 – online at *JStor*.

[26] In Muslim societies, which certainly support businesses, and carry on international trade, have never had anything comparable to a legal corporation. This would be an interesting study.

[27] Bruce R. Scott, *The Concept of Capitalism* (Berlin: Springer Verlag, 2009).

[28] See for example, Charles Hughes Smith, "Social Fractals and the Corruption of America," in *OfTwoMinds.com*, February 8, 2012; "Mike P. Sinn, "Financial Sector Costs Us More Than Any Other Sector in the Economy" in *Thinkbynumbers.org*, April 11, 2012; Simon Johnson, "The Quiet Coup," in *The Atlantic*, May 1, 2009; and Matt Taibbi, "Secrets and Lies of the Bailout," in *Rolling Stone*, January 4, 2013.

[29] Amartya Sen, *Development as Freedom* (New.York.: Anchor Books, 1999).

[30] For a favorable analysis, see R.E. Baldwin, H. Braconier and R.Forslid, "Multinationals, Endogenous Growth and Technological Spillovers," Discussion Paper #2155 (1999), Centre for Economic Policy Research, London. For an unfavorable analysis, see World Trade Organization, "Trade Liberalization Statistics" at *www.gatt.org/trastat_e.html*.

[31] *Cf. Wikipedia*, "Multinational corporation" and "Globalization".

[32] A. Maddison, "The Assessment: The Twentieth Century – Achievements, Failures, Lessons," in *Oxford Review of Economic Policy*, Winter 1999.

[33] Most of this section comes from articles in *Wikipedia*, under headings of "Marketing" and "History of marketing," especially the "Timeline of Innovation" (2008).

[34] The topic of governmental 'spying' on citizens for reasons of security is a current very emotional topic of discussion, in news and political conversations,

but to date the invasiveness of commercial interests into personally targeted 'profiling' of potential buyers has continued with only minimal awareness or complaint.

[35] Adam Davidson and Alex Blumberg, "The Giant Pool of Money," This America Life, Part 355, May 9, 2008 on WBEZ Radio Chicago (and other NPR stations).

[36] Cf. Edmund Conway, in *The Telegraph*, August 8, 2009, citing figures from the IMF. I haven't seen a recent update.

[37] Cf. Mark Landler, *New York Times*, April 21, 2009, citing IMF figures.

[38] See Matthew Berg, "The Spinning Top Economy," in *New Economic Perspectives* blog, Feb 25, 2013.

[39] We will examine oligarchy in Chapter 5 below.

[40] See Gary Rivlin, "How Wall Street Defanged Dodd-Frank." *The Nation*, May 20, 2013; and Bill Black, on the gutting of the Dodd-Frank bill, in his interview by *The Real News Network*, November 1, 2013.

[41] Cf. Simon Johnson article, "The Quiet Coup".

[42] Michael Sinn, *thinkbynumbers.org* blog, April 11, 2012.

[43] Cf. Ira M. Price, "The Schools of the Sons of the Prophets" (Chicago: University of Chicago Press, 1889) 244-249, in *JStorr*.

[44] I.e., one percent monthly interest.

[45] Cf. Strong's concordance, e.g. in the website *www.QBible.com*.

[46] See *Wikipedia*, "New Testament," especially sections on "Books", "Authors", and "Dates of composition".

[47] Seven is the divine number, i.e. completion or perfection. Seventy times seven is poetic hyperbole; it means infinitely.

[48] See footnote to *Deut.* 4:13 in *The King James Study Bible* (Nashville, TN: Thomas Nelson, 1988).

[49] Cf. Geoffrey P. Miller, *The Ways of a King: Legal and Political Ideas in the Bible* (Gottingen: Vandenhoeck and Ruprecht, 2011).

[50] 45 On this topic, see the stories about David and Bathsheba (2 *Sam.*:11:5); and about Ahab and Jezebel, and coveting the vineyard of Naboth (1 *Kings* 21).

[51] Barnes' Notes on the Bible, which can be found in biblehub.com/commentaries/exodus/20-17.

[52] From what I can tell, the ratio of the two debts is more than 500,000 to 1. See the website of Jona Lendering, at *livius.org*, on "weights and measures" at various historical periods.

[53] The English word "talent" gained this secondary meaning of its Latin root in medieval times, because of this parable.

[54] Cf. Sigmund Freud, *Totem and Taboo* (New York: Moffat Yard and Company, 1918) – first German edition 1913; and *Group Psychology and the Analysis of the Ego* (New York: Boni & Liveright, 1922) – first German edition 1921.

[55] For a summary of Girard's ideas I recommend James G. Williams (ed), *A Girard Reader*, (New York: Crossroad Publishing Co., 1996).

[56] Cf. a video by Jonathan Rose "Who was Swedenborg? What should I Read?" Swedenborg Foundation, 2013.

[57] Cf. Karen Armstrong *A History of God* (New York: Ballentine,1993), and *The Bible: A Biography* (New York: Atlantic Monthly Press, 2007); and Elaine Pagels *Revelations: Visions, Prophecy, and Politics in the Book of Revelations* (New York: Viking, 2012).

[58] E.g. see Soren Kierkegaard, *Philosophhical Fragments*, D. F. Swenson trans (Princeton: Princeton University Press, 1962) p. 31 – 36. I don't like Kierkegaard's discounting of reason (in keeping with his Calvinist background, and his 'existential' orientation), but he has wonderful insights.

[59] 1986 interview by Claudia Dreifus, by *The Progressive magazine*.

[60] Jeffrey A. Winters, *Oligarchy* (New York: Cambridge U. Press, 2011).

[61] Aristotle, *Politics* III: 7.

[62] At scribd.com/doc/82492158/Respect-Relativism-and-Cultures-of Honor.

[63] From G. W. Domhoff, "Wealth, Income and Power" in *whorulesamerica.net* (at University of California at Santa Clara).

[64] Study by M. I. Norton and D. Ariely, "Building a better America – one wealth quintile at a time" in *Perspectives on Psychological Science* (2010), cited in Domhoff.

[65] E.g. see Zanny Bedoes, "Inequality and the World Economy," in *The Econo*mist, October 13, 2012.

[66] Warren Buffet, "Stop Coddling the Super Rich," in *New York Times* Opinion Pages, Aug 14,2011.

[67] Andrew Carnegie, *The Gospel of Wealth*, 1889.

[68] 63 Joseph Stiglitz, "Tax System Stacked Against the 99%" in *New York Times* Opinion Pages, April 15, 2013.

[69] See G. W. Domhoff, "Wealth, Income and Power" in *whorulesamerica.net* (at U. of California, Santa Clara), p. 5.

[70] "Pete Peterson Has Won," in neweconomicperspectives.org for October 26, 2012.

[71] Jeffrey A. Winters, *Oligarchy* (New York: Cambridge University Press, 2011), p. 237 -242.

[72] Cited in Winters, *Oligarchy*, p. 234.

[73] *Oligarchy*, p. 233.

[74] *Oligarchy*, p. 236.

[75] *Oligarchy*, pp. 223-225.

[76] *Oligarchy*, p. 221.

[77] *Oligarchy*, p. 245.

[78] See Thomas Piketty, Emanuel Saez, "Income Inequality in the United States, 1913-1998" in *Quarterly Journal of Economics* 118:1 (2003), updated and cited by Winters, p. 215.

[79] See Jacques Ellul, *Propaganda: The Formation of Men's Attitudes* (New York, Vintage, 1965).

[80] *Wikipedia*, "Socio-economic mobility in the United States".

[81] Jason DeParle, "Harder for Americans to Rise from Lower Rungs," *New York Times* article, Jan 4, 2012.

[82] Isabel V.Sawhill and John E. Morton, "Economic Mobility: Is the American Dream Alive and Well?" Brookings Institution/ Research (May 2007).

[83] See Vasia Panousi, Ivan Vidangos, Shanti Ramnath, Jason DeBacker, and Bradley Heim, "Inequality Rising and Permanent Over Past Two Decades," Brookings Papers on Economic Activity, Brookings Institution (Spring 2013).

[84] The poll results during this period were quite controversial, and seemed to encourage differing interpretations. See Greg Sargent, "Sixth national poll shows majority support for ending tax cuts for rich," *Washington Post*, September 14, 2010.

[85] For an analysis of the GFC, see Eduardo Pol, "Understanding the Global Financial Crisis," Cambridge University, October 2009.

[86] Matt Taibbi, "Secrets and Lies of the Bailout" in *Rolling Stone*, January 4, 2013.

[87] See news item in *The Washington Post* for June 13, 2013.

[88] Cf. David Indiviglio, "12 industries that are actually growing", *The Atlantic*, Feb 2,2011; "Top 50 fastest growing industries – 2010-2020", in

careerinfonet.org; and Bureau of Labor Statistics (BLS) Office of occupational statistics and employment projections – Occupational Outlook Handbook.

[89] Christopher Chantrill, at *USGovernmentspending.com* (including federal, state, transfer and local spending)

[90] E.g. *Wikipedia*, and *About.com*. Chantrill's interactive website format is very convenient.

[91] 86 Cf. R. R. Kelley and Raymond Fabius MD, "A Path to Eliminate" 3.6 Trillion in Wasteful Healthcare Spending," White Paper from Thompson-Reuters Health Care Analytics, June 2010.

[92] Diane Heldt, "Economists: Student loan debt a concern, but is it the next bubble?" *The Gazette*, Iowa City, May 5, 2013.

[93] 88 Cf. Ross DeVol, Kevin Klowden, Armen Bedroussian, and Benjamin Yeo, "North America's High-Tech Economy: The Geography of Knowledge-Based Industries," an Executive Summary from the Miliken Institute, June 2009.

[94] See *Wikipedia*, "Labor unions in the United States".

[95] Cf. *Wikipedia* article: "Right-to-work law;" and editorial "Meet the billionaires behind No Rights at Work" in *Teamster Nation*, January 27, 2013.

[96] See Rasmussen Reports poll, cited in *Wikipedia* article "Right-to-work law"; and *New York Times* article "Share of the workforce in a union falls to a 97-year low: 11.3%", in NYT Business Day, January 24, 2013.

[97] See Economic Policy Institute, (EPI) "Resources on unions and the economy;" and discussions about the economic effects of minimum wage laws.

[98] J. D. Alt, "Let it be Done – An Alternative Narrative for Building what America Needs," in *neweconomicperspectives.org*, June 17, 2013.

[99] See *Wikipedia*, "Growth in a Time of Debt;" and John Cassidy, "The Reinhart and Rogoff Controversy: A Summing Up" in *The New Yorker*, April 29, 2013.

[100] Thomas Herndon, Michael Ash and Robert Pollin, "Does High Public Debt Consistently Stifle Economic Growth? A Critique of Reinhart and Rogoff" in

Political Economy Research Institute, University of Massachusetts Amherst, April15, 2013.

[101] *Wikipedia*, "Timeline of US military operations."

[102] Christopher Hedges, *The Death of the Liberal Class* (New York: Nation Books, 2010).

[103] *Wikipedia*, "Military budget of the United States."

[104] Cf Kimberly Amadeo, "Current U.S. Military Budget: How Defense Spending Affects the Economy" in *About.com*. Also see "FY 2013 U.S. Federal Government Budget," in *About.com*: US Economy.

[105] This is according to an article in *The Economist* June 8, 2011.

[106] *Wikipedia*, "United States Department of Defense."

[107] *Wikipedia*, "United States Military Pay," especially "Base Pay Tables" taken from DOD sites, included in this source.

[108] See Lawrence Mishel and Natalie Sabadish, "CEO Pay and the Top 1%: How Executive Compensation and Financial Sector Pay Have Fueled Income Inequality," in Economic Policy Institute report on Inequality and Poverty, May 2, 2012.

[109] 104 Milton Friedman, "The Social Responsibility of Business is to Increase Its Profits," *New York Times* magazine, September 13, 1970 (just before the gold standard was dropped by President Nixon.)

[110] Cf. Libby Sander, "Freshman Survey: This Year Even More Focused On Jobs", *Chronicle of Higher Education*, January 224, 2013.

[111] Christopher Hedges, *The Death of the Liberal Class* (N.Y.: Perseus/Nation Books, 2010.

[112] Charles Hughes Smith, "Social Fractals and the Corruption of America," in *oftwominds.com*, Februar 8, 2012.

[113] See Matt Taibbi, "Secrets and Lies of the Bank Bailout;" *Rolling Stone*; and Simon Johnson, "The Quiet Coup" referred to earlier.

[114] See M. J. Sparacio, "The Devil in Virgina," Doctoral Dissertation submission to Virginia Polytechnic Institute, 2010. He also presents an interesting take on religious superstitions in the early Virginia colonies.

[115] James W. J. Bowden's blog, *Parliamentum.org*. (Canadian) "George III, Parliament and the Loss of the American Colonies," August 9, 2011. This author also discusses the relative responsibilities of the King and the Parliament in the American revolution.

[116] See *Wikipedia*, "Religion and politics in the United States."

[117] It was written in 1892, but only adopted by Congress in 1942. See *Wikipedia*, "Pledge of Allegiance".

[118] The phrase was first used by Jefferson in a letter to some of his Baptist supporters in Danbury, Connecticut. It was also used in 1947, by Justice Black, arguing for the majority opinion, and Justice Rutledge for the minority, in *Everson v. Board of Education*. Cf. *Wikipedia* article "Everson v. Board of Education".

[119] Steven Waldman, *Founding Faith* (New York: Random House, 2012).

[120] This is a principle of classical liberal democratic philosophy, well stated in *On Liberty* by John Stuart Mill, where he addressed the 'modern' problem of 'dictatorship by the many' that arises in democratic societies.

[121] See, e.g. *The Federalist*; and Colleen Sheehan, "Madison v. Hamilton: The Battle over Republicanism and the Role of Public Opinion," *The American Political Science Review*, (Aug 2004), 405-424.

[122] Excerpted in *Wikipédia* article, "Federalist Papers".

[123] Letter to John Wise in Francis N. Thorpe, ed., "A Letter from Jefferson on the Political Parties, 1798," *American Historical Review* v.3#3 (April 1898) pp 488–89, cited in *Wikipedia* article, "First Party System."

[124] Catholics were excluded from British rule by law until 2013!

[125] Cf. Murray Edelman, *Symbolic Uses of Politics* (Urbana/Chicago: University of Illinois Press, 1964); and *Constructing the Political Spectacle* (Chicago: University of Chicago Press, 1988).

[126] See Dan Kervick, "The social dimension of prosperity," in *NewEconomicPerspectives.org*, December 3, 2012.

[127] See L. Randall Wray, *Modern Money Theory*; Dale Pierce, "Modern Monetary Theory – An Introduction: Part 3" in *neweconomicperspectives.org* for April 24, 2013; and other writers at *New Economic Perspectives*, for ideas that inform this discussion of Modern Money.

[128] Actually, this business of "clearing", which is completed at the end of each day, is very complicated, involving intermediary agencies like the Clearing House Interbank Payment System (CHIPS) and communications with regional Federal Reserve banks, in order to make the operations efficient and smooth running. But the basic process is as I have summarized in this section. For a more exact, but still clear description, see Dan Kervick, "Do Banks Create Money from Thin Air?" at *neweconomicperspectives.org*, for June 3, 2013.

[129] This idea, that currency is a 'token' is sometimes called "Chartalism," from the Latin *carta* – "token."

[130] This distinction between Treasury Department minting of coins and Federal Reserve printing of bills often gets into current disputes about how to pay of the national debt, and how to avoid raising the debt limit. See *Wikipedia* article, "Trillion Dollar Coin;" and *Bloomberg Report* blog for January 14, 2013, "Economics is Platinum: What the Trillion Dollar Coin Teaches Us."

[131] L. Randall Wray, *Modern Money Theory*, p. 278.

[132] Dale Pierce uses the terms 'tax credit' and 'IOU' in "Modern Money Theory – An Introduction: Part 3" at *New Economic Perspectives*, April 24, 2013. Randall Wray calls money in any form 'debt,' and a 'token' that can be 'redeemed' (e.g. in *Modern Money Theory*, sec. 8.3 and 5.3) which is what I would emphasize.

[133] Dan Kervik, "Do Banks Create Money from Thin Air?" *New Economic Perspectives*, June 3, 2013; also see Randall Wray, *Modern Money Theory*, Ch. 3: Domestic Monetary System.

[134] Hyman Minsky, *Stabilizing an Unstable Economy* (New Haven and London: Yale University Press, 1986) 228, cited in Randall Wray, *Modern Money Theory*, p. 272.

[135] Ron Paul is one of the politically high-profile 'gold bugs'. About the inadvisability of the return to gold standard, see Matthew Obrien, "Why the Gold Standard is the World's Worst Economic Idea," in *The Atlantic*, August 26, 2012.

[136] Since the 1931 depression, J. M Keynes and others had argued against the gold standard, and its causing liquidity problems. Cf. e.g. *Wikipedia* article, "The Gold Standard".

[137] See *Wikipedia*, under "The Gold Standard".

[138] 132 Christine Desan, "Coin Reconsidered" *Theoretical Inquiries in Law* Vol. 11 (2012), 361- 409, from the precis (my emphasis). See also her video lecture (Seminar 5: Constitutional History) in the Modern Money and Public Purpose series of talks, sponsored by Columbia University Law School, which is on-going, and available on the Internet at *modernmoneyandpublicpurpose.com*.

[139] See *federalreserve.gov/faqs/currency* "How much US currency is in Circulation?"; and Wikipedia, "Economy of the United States".

[140] Cf. Julia Werdigier, "London Wants to Tap Chinese Currency Market," in New York Times Dealbook at *dealbook.nytimes.com*, January 16, 2012.

[141] Cf. "The Spinning Top Economy" in *New Economic Perspectives*, February25, 2013.

[142] John Maynard Keynes, *General Theory of Interest, Employment and Money*, 1936 ; L. Randall Wray, "Money in Finance", in Jan Toporowsky, & Joe Michell (eds) *Handbook of Critical Issues in Finance*, Edward Elgar Publishing, 2012 Ch. 33 (pp.243-253) in Google Books.

[143] Cf. Wray, *Modern Money Theory*, especially pp. 6-14.

[144] *Collected Writings of John Maynard Keynes*, Vol 21, quoted in John Quiqqin, *Zombie Economics: How Dead Ideas Still Walk Among Us* (Princeton, NJ: Princeton University Press, 2010, Ch 6, "Expansionary Austerity." See also Paul

Krugman, "Keynes Was Right," NYT Opinion, Dec 29, 2010. See also Jeffrey Frankel, "Reinhart-Rogoff controversy," at *econointersect.com* for May 30, 2013; and "Monetary Alchemy, Fiscal Science," at Jeffrey Frankel's Weblog for Jan 16, 2013.

[145] Actually, Friedman originally was close to the MMT viewpoint about national debt, and to those like Keynes and Abba Lerner who preceded them. L. R. Wray discusses Friedman's 1948 article, "A Monetary and Fiscal Framework for Economic Stability" in *Modern Money Theory*, pp. 195 - 197.

[146] Frank Newman, *Freedom From National Debt*, cited by Stephanie Kelton in "Former Deputy Secretary of the US Treasury Department Endorses Modern Money Theory (MMT)", in *neweconomicperspectives.org*, July16, 2013.

[147] For a classic in modern ethics on this topic, see John Rawls, *A Theory of Justice* (Cambridge, MA: Harvard University Press, 1971); and a brief restatement of his views in "Justice as Fairness: Political not Metaphysical", in *Philosophy and Public Affairs* 14 (Summer 1985), 223 – 281. For an opposing view, cf. Robert Nozick, *Anarchy, State and Utopia* (New York: Basic Books, 1974).

[148] Cf. John Dewey, "Democracy and Educational Administration," in *School and Society* XLV (April 3, 1937).

[149] E.g., Karl Popper, *Open Society and Its Enemies*, Vol. 1: The Spell of Plato (London: Routledge, 1945).

[150] Paul Krugman, "War on the Unemployed," *Wall Street Journal* opinion editorial essay, June 30, 2013.

[151] See L. Randall Wray, "Public Service Employment: Full Employment Without Inflation," Working Paper #3, January 2000, Center for Full Employment and Price Stability, University of Missouri at Kansas City for most of the ideas here. See also L. Randall Wray, *Modern Money Theory*, Ch. 7; Fadhel Kaboub, "Employment Guarantee Programs: A Survey of Theories and Policy Experiences," Working Paper #498, Levy Economics Institute, 2007; and Dan Kervick, "The Emancipation of the Unemployed"; at *NewEconomicPerspectives.org*, September 3, 2012. See also Philip Pilkington, "Labour's Forgotten Jobs Guarantee," *Monitor*, June 7, 2013; and Hyman Minsky (posthumous), *Ending Poverty: Jobs, Not Welfare*, Levy Economics Institute , 2013. Lastly, see 'The Parable of the Workers in the Vineyard,' *Matt.* 20:6.

[152] At www.modernmoneynetwork.org.

[153] *Wikipedia*, "Chemtrail conspiracy theory".

[154] www.globalskywatch.com.

[155] See Ivan Illich, *Deschooling Society* (London: Marion Boyars, 1970).

[156] Cf. Harvard Health Literacy Studies, Dr. Rima Rudd.

[157] See National Public Radio news item, "Penn State to Penalize Workers Who Refuse Health Screenings", August 2, 2013.

[158] Reuters, "Republicans and Democrats Diverge on Health Care Issues," March 20, 2008 (cited in Elizabeth Docteur and Robert A. Berenson, "How Does the Quality of U.S. Health Care Compare Internationally?" Robert Wood Johnson Foundation, Urban Institute report, August 2009 at *www.urban.org*. For a view from the conservative political perspective, see H.E. Frech, Stephen T. Parente and John Huff, "US Health Care: A Reality Check on Cross-Country Comparisons" July 11, 2012 in *American Enterprise Institute*.

[159] Elizabeth Docteur and Robert A. Berenson, "How Does the Quality of U.S. Health Care Compare Internationally?" Robert Wood Johnson Foundation, Urban Institute report, August 2009 *at www.urban.org*.

[160] Cf World Health Organization list in 2011.

[161] OECD Health Data report for 2012, "U.S. Health care system from an international perspective." For an assessment by States of the United States, see The Commonwealth Fund, "State Scorecard on Health System Performance" annual series.

[162] A recent news item reported that Mexicans consume twice the number of sugary drinks per capita that Americans do. They are almost a staple of Mexican food, from childhood up. In one current advertising campaign, Coca-Cola has offered to put up free road signs that announce the name of the next small village that a tourist is approaching. The iconic *Coke* logo appears on each one.

¹⁶³ Elizabeth Rosenthal, "For Medical Tourists, Simple Math" in *New York Times*, August 4, 2013. For an academic assessment of how to save money in the system, see R. Kelley, "A Path to Eliminating $3.6 Trillion in Wasteful Healthcare Spending," White Paper of Thompson-Reuters, June 2010.

¹⁶⁴ An old folk song, whose title 'Kum ba ya' is Gulla language for 'Come by here.'

¹⁶⁵ Eduardo Porter, NYT Obituaries, March 6, 2004.

¹⁶⁶ For those interested in further study, here are some other relevant sources. Ed Diener and Eunkook Suh, "Measuring Quality of Life: Economic, social and subjective indicators," in *Social Indicators Research* Vol 40 (Netherlands: Kluwer Academic Publishers, 1997) pp. 189-216; "The Economist Intelligence Unit's Quality of Life Index," 2005, from *The Economist*; "QOLIndex: 194 Countries Ranked and Rated" in *International Living*, 2010; Heinrich-Heinz Noll, "Social Indicators and QOL Research: Background, Achievements and Current Trends," in *Advances in Sociological Knowledge Over Half a Century* (Wiesbaden: VS Verlag fur Sozialwissenschaften, 2004) 151-181; Amartya Sen, *Development as Freedom* (Oxford, UK: Oxford University Press, 1999); and Marc Miringoff and Marque-Luisa Miringoff, *The Social Health of the Nation: How America is Really Doing* (New York: Oxford Press, 1999).

¹⁶⁷ Plato, *Meno*, 97b-98a.

¹⁶⁸ *Meno* 80e.

¹⁶⁹ *Meno* 84b.

¹⁷⁰ Plato, *Apology*, 23b (Rouse translation).

¹⁷¹ As a disclaimer, I admit my ideas about knowledge here are pretty much 'classical', especially the 'justified true belief' ideas that follow Plato in his *Meno* and *Theaetetus*. These ideas have been strongly critiqued by 20th century linguists. See Standford Encyclopedia of Philosophy article "The Analysis of Knowledge" at *www.plato.stanford.edu*.

¹⁷² Cf. Bill Casselman's "Words of the World" and "Canadian Word of the Day" under "school," at *billcasselman.com*.

[173] Much of the following is based on various articles in *Wikipedia* about "History of education in the United States."

[174] Cf. e.g. *Wikipedia*, "History of education in the United States".

[175] In his book, *The Triumph of Conservatism* (New York: Free Press, 1963), historian Gabriel Kolko objects to calling this era "progressive" at all, since its major developments were to serve mainly upper class economic interests.

[176] See *Wikipedia* on "John Amos Comenius".

[177] See *Wikipedia* article, "John Amos Comenius" and Jacques Barzun "John Amos Comenius" in *From Dawn to Decadence: 500 Years of Western Cultural Life* (New York: Harper Collins, 2000), p. 180-182.

[178] Cited in Jacques Barzun, *From Dawn to Decadence*, p. 181.

[179] From Dawn to Decadence, p. 180.

[180] Ivan Illich, *Deschooling Society* (London: Marion Boyars, 1970), p. 111.

[181] See also Peter McLaren Life in Schools: An Introduction to Critical Pedagogy in the Foundations of Education (New York: Longman,1998); and Jonathan Kozol, Savage Inequalities: Children in America's Schools (New York: Crown Publishers, 1991.

[182] Peter McLaren Life in Schools: An Introduction to Critical Pedagogy in the Foundations of Education (New York: Longman, 1998).

[183] E.g. Jean Piaget, Jerome Bruner, Benjamin Bloom, L.S. Vygotsky, and K. Patricia Cross.

[184] Cf. Dan Kervick, "The Social Dimension of Prosperity" at *New Economic Perspectives*, December 3, 2012.

[185] See ProjectGutenberg.org.

[186] See www.TED.com.

[187] See www.khanacademy.org.

[188] 183 See *New. York Times/ Education* article, by Tamar Lewin for May 2, 2012, "Harvard and M.I.T. Team Up To Offer Free Online Courses."

[189] See Sean Coughlan, "UK Enters Global Online University Race," BBC News/ Education, September 18, 2013.

Since I first wrote this book, another online source – *Libre Texts* – has appeared that is too new to allow for a confident judgment, but looks promising. It has free courses, tests, and study aids for advanced study in all the STEM fields, as well as humanities, and social sciences. Its motto: "Free the Textbook!". The website describes it as a "multi-institutional collaboration to improve education at all levels of higher learning by developing open access resources".

[190] Cf. Carlyle's 1849 tract entitled "Occasional Discourse on the Negro Question".

[191] See An Essay on the Principle of Population, first published in 1798.

[192] As of May, 2013, in Chicago, over a third of mortgaged properties are still under water, six years after the housing market turned down.

[193] In his 'Sermon on the Mount,' Jesus identifies three degrees of wrong doing associated with three degree of law broken (civil, religious and divine): the Judge, the Council and Hell (not God). See *Matthew* 5:22.

[194] See, Immanuel Kant, *Critique of Pure Reason*, N. K. Smith trans. (London: Macmillan,1929), e.g. the section on "The Distinction between Pure and Empirical Knowledge," pp. 41-45.

[195] Aristotle, *Nichomachean Ethics*, Bk. V, Ch. VI.